THE
COMPASS
OF
NOW

By

DDNARD

CONTENTS

FORM 4 PURPOSES AND VALUES 94

Part

1

REFLECT

STOP A MOMENT...
AND REFLECT

Draw in a deep breath ... release it slowly.
Observe the feeling in your heart.
Is this heart becoming weary?

Notice how your eyes keep on reading these letters, not wanting to pause even a moment to see how you feel.

Our mind keeps on running in and out, up and down. Moving, looking, listening, thinking, sensing—hoping to feel better.

In search of true happiness, we do more ... see more ... earn more ... have more—but true, lasting happiness never comes.

We may drain ourselves from the day we were born to the day we die. Unless we actually understand certain life truths ... understand the process of building within ourselves a firm, long-lasting happiness, any life goals we set are not the destinations we long for.

Where do we really want to go?

THE WISE
GRANDMA

There once lived an old lady whose two grandsons had recently moved in with her. Every night after work, the two young men went out to enjoy themselves at the mall, the bar, or the movie theatre —leaving their grandmother alone at home. When the grandmother told them they should stop going out so much, both grandsons retorted that they worked hard every day and deserved to go out and enjoy themselves.

> Late one night, the two grandsons returned from a pleasurable evening to find their grandmother walking around in front of the house, stopping now and then to bend over and look closely at the ground. She had lost her sewing needle, she told them.
> "Where exactly do you think you dropped it, Grandma? We'll help you find it right away!"

"I dropped it somewhere around my bed," Grandma quickly answered.
"Huh? And then you came here in front of the house to find your needle, Grandma?" they asked, incredulous.
"Well, this area is well-lit by the street light. It's the easiest place to find my needle," Grandma explained.

> At that, both grandsons fell to the ground and rolled in laughter.
> "Grandma, dear, how did you become so confused? You dropped your needle in your bedroom, yet you come to look for it out here, under this street light!"

Grandma straightaway replied, "My dear boys, and why won't I find it? It's just like you two. You lose your happiness in your heart and then you go looking for it at the bar, the theatre, and the mall. Did you find yours?"

Fire In The Heart

Have you ever seen the fire within your heart? The pushing force inside that drives you to make a phone call, restlessly browse on social network, turn on the television, go out, open the refrigerator, or think a certain thought?

This restlessness in our heart is the driving force behind all we say, think, and do. We do things hoping that this restlessness will disappear and we will be contented.

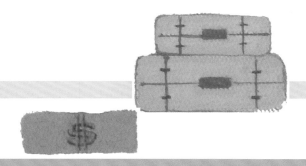

When we were infants, this inner force drove each of us to get our milk bottle, to raise up our arms to be hugged and held, to reach out for toys—to get whatever we needed to feel secure and comfortable.

Observe your mind. See how your thoughts and feelings arise. Be aware of them before they turn to words and actions. Where are your thoughts leading you?

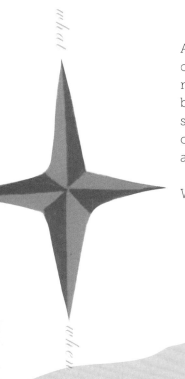

As we grow older, we have the same impulses, only now the toys have become bigger and more expensive. We make more money, build bigger homes, buy better cars. We strive for more power, security, significance, excitement, achievement, fame, and, of course, love and companionship.

What do we get?

We believe we'll be happy and fulfilled when we reach our goals. But happiness somehow is always ahead of us. There are always the next goals to be achieved with the promising hope that life will be fulfilled.

But no matter how much we have, the void inside is never filled.

Humans have freedom. We have the freedom to choose our feelings, thoughts, and actions, no matter what we are facing.

Humans are different from animals because we have self-awareness. We are able to look inside to see how we feel, to be above our feelings, not controlled by them.

To be self-aware is to observe our body and mind. To notice that everything we do in our life, from breathing to eating, everything, is to keep us away from pain. We breathe in and have to breathe out, eat and excrete, have companionships and possessions to comfort us, moving away from pain towards well-being.

And what is us? Us is our body and mind. To be aware of our body and mind helps us to see how anguish arises and passes away.

We can develop awareness of our mind, eyes, ears, nose, tongue, and bodily senses, to truly realize what is happening inside and outside of us now, so that we can wisely choose our reaction to each sensation experienced.

We humans are born to develop ourselves through the practice of mindfulness. We are capable of sensing ourselves — to be aware of now, not consumed by thoughts, memories and feelings. We can have them, acknowledge them, and not be consumed by them. We are capable of deciding how to respond in thoughts, feelings, words, and actions.

However, our schooling and training focus on reading, writing, and other skill sets connected to getting a job and being able to take care of our material needs and wants. Our life curriculum does not include drills on how to keep our mind free from the control of instincts and habits. Priorities at school are not to train us to cultivate happiness in ourselves, to develop our inner human potential, to be free.

Half our life is spent trying to find something to do with the time we have rushed through life trying to save.

Will Rogers

We generally grow up doing just what everyone else is doing, without really considering: What am I doing? Why am I doing it this way? We hurry along, never stopping long enough to reflect, competing with each other at school and then later at work. And we feel the pressure to marry and have children by a certain age. But of course we do not hurry to grow old, get sick, or die. Then it suddenly hits us that this will happen. We will grow old, begin to ail ... and soon no longer exist.

And so, imagine one person inexorably racing through life towards his death, never stopping long enough to consider: Is there more to life than getting rich? Is there more to it than raising a family, performing some good deeds, committing a few bad ones, laughing and crying, experiencing happiness and suffering — and then dying? This rat race that we live in simply because it's what everyone else is doing: Is this right? Is this good enough? Can this path truly bring us sustainable happiness? What is the purpose of life that we can experience now, not after death?

About the time one learns to make the most of life, most of it is gone.

Anonymous

The Compass of NOW

Before continuing this journey, let us stop ... and reflect: All my life what have I been doing—and why? Try writing down your observations. They may look something like this ...

what

Endlessly fixating on increasing the amount of money in my bank account in order to attain a feeling of security—though the stress never lessens.

Elbowing my way through my career hoping that when I become number one, I'll attain personal contentment—but success seems to move further away each time I move closer.

Working from dawn till dusk in order for my family to live comfortably and securely—but hardly finding the time and energy to enjoy myself with my family.

why

Enjoying myself in every possible way to keep my spirits elevated—but then feeling even more empty, downhearted, and apprehensive.

Stop ... and reflect one random second in your day: what am I doing—and why?

Chat idly with friends on the phone or Facebook because I just cannot keep still.

Criticizing others in order to make myself feel better than them. Have full list of activities all the time in order to make myself feel useful and valuable—while becoming more weary, more irritable, and more depleted.

Watch and observe closely each moment over a period of time: What am I about to do—and why? Follow your emotions ... look into your ever-changing mind and patiently, sense the driving force at work within.

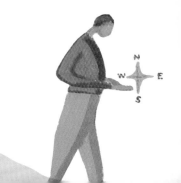

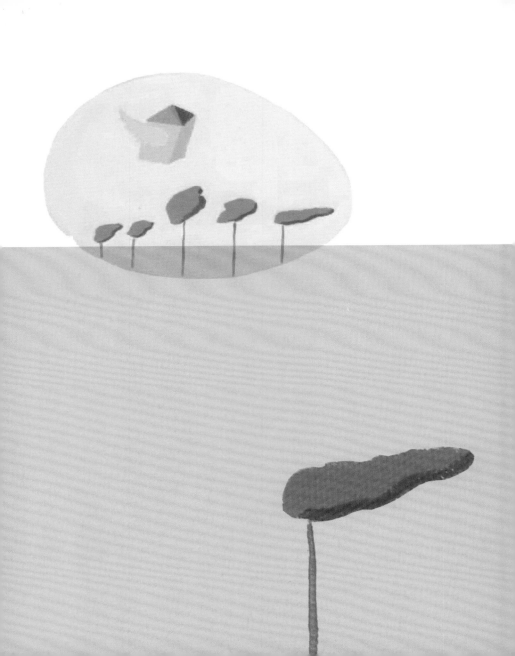

Part 2 CHECK LIFE
TRUTHS

Swimology

Once upon a time, there was a university professor who traveled on a ship. Every day the professor talked to an old man who had been a sailor all his life and had not attended any school.

One day, the professor asked the old sailor, "Do you know anything about geology?"

"Oh, Professor! I never went to school. I don't know geology." The old sailor replied in sorrow for his ignorance.

MY HOUSE
MY FAMILY
MY HUSBAND
MY .....

"What a shame!" The professor declared. "You worked on this beautiful ship, but you don't know anything about geology. You have wasted one-third of your life."

The sailor walked back to his room, sad in the knowledge that he had wasted a third of his life.

The next day, the professor asked him, "Do you know anything about oceanology?"

"Oh, professor! I didn't go to school. I don't know oceanology," the old sailor replied, sorrowful for his lack of knowledge.

"What a shame!" the professor asserted. "You worked on this beautiful ship, yet you don't know anything about oceanology. You have wasted two-thirds of your life."

The sailor walked back to his room saddened to know that he had wasted two-thirds of his life.

The next day the sailor ran to the professor's cabin and asked anxiously, "Professor, do you know any swimology?"

"What swimology?" the professor replied, annoyed. "I don't waste my time with that kind of thing. I have more important things to study."

The old sailor replied, "Well, if you don't know any swimology, I am afraid you will lose your entire life because our ship is sinking right now. Pity! If you had learned swimology, among all that other knowledge of yours, you could swim to shore and survive."

How many times in our life have we learned so many things except how to get ourselves out of misery when things do not go our way?

There are times we might have asked ourselves: Why should we learn and practice swimming when we've never come close to drowning?

Why learn inner happiness when we've been leading happy, enjoyable life?

We've all known people who have been kind and generous their whole lives ... people who do no harm to anyone—except to themselves.

No matter how goodhearted they are, when they lose their jobs, lose their loved ones, get sick, get slandered or libeled, don't get what they want or get what they don't want—good people suffer.

No matter how good a person is, he or she will experience pain in life from time to time.

Some people may choose to surrender and accept that it is natural to feel bad when we get what we don't want or when we are sick or have suffered the loss of a loved one or things we love.

Two thousand six hundred years ago, one man stood up against the belief that we cannot be free from the suffering of old age, sickness, death, and being parted from things that are dear to us.

Prince Siddhartha, the Buddha, put the right question to the world: Why not?

Why can't we be free from the suffering of birth, death, sickness, aging, or losing loved ones and things we care for? Are we just helpless victims of life, with our feelings tossed up and down through life cycles? The Buddha asked the right question and experimented the right way till he found the path of mindfulness, which gives us freedom to end our suffering, to be free and above our own emotions and feelings. We have freedom to choose how we feel no matter what happens.

The Uncertainty of Life

At twenty years of age, a young lady completed a master degree in business administration and another master degree in Economics from the University of London.

On the day she graduated, she reflected on herself, *I've gained great knowledge of the world, I have a strong sense of purpose and direction, my parents are proud of me, and I am a good daughter and an excellent achiever. Life will be great.*

Two years later, at twenty-two years of age, she bought herself a new Mercedes-Benz. Driving her new car to work, she felt neutral inside. This made her stop and ponder.

There are things that we want because we think that when we have them, we'll feel truly happy. But when what we longed for arrives, happiness and excitement seem to fade away so quickly. So what now? What will bring true, long-lasting joy to our soul?

But the questions weren't strong enough to send her on a search for answers.

She continued moving through life, full of love and energy.

At twenty-five, she started her own business with partners, got married, and had a baby while her business prospered.

The moment she glowed with pride in her accomplishment, the moment she felt the world was in her hands—in the blink of an eye, she was taken over and lost her entire business.

Unable to face anyone, she retreated to her parents' home in the countryside.

Waking up the next morning, her whole body felt as if every drop of blood had been drained out. She didn't want to move or get out of bed. Her family tried to comfort her with, "You'll get over it. This kind of thing happens to everyone." But it didn't soothe the pain.

She thought to herself, *All our lives we're all taught to be good girls, good boys, work hard, play hard, and get good jobs. We're told that if we do things we love well, with good energy and at the right time, we will be successful and happy. But what if being good and doing the right things are not enough to have good and happy life? Then what?*

Looking at her nine-month-old baby, her parents, and her husband, who tried to comfort her in every way, she asked herself, *Am I going to let my son have a weak mother, who hides herself away in a comfort zone?*

At that moment, she felt lightning strike in her heart. She saw why she kept on giving excuses to everyone about why it was best for her to start a small business in the countryside with her parents. SHE HAD FEARS! She had a fear of not being as successful as she used to be and a fear that any new business she started might not become as big and famous as her last one. She saw her fears.

One thing about fear is, once you see and recognize it, it doesn't seem as scary anymore.

She jumped on a plane that afternoon, called a meeting with her teams and started a new company. Within one month, she opened up three new branches, and her business became as big as it used to be.

Less than a month later, her big family agreed to gather and celebrate the new year's holiday on the beautiful island of Phuket, Thailand.

Arriving at the holiday home on the island, Christmas and New Year's holiday music was everywhere. Excited and happy, the young woman had just picked up her child and the car key, ready to go pick up her husband, when her mother strode into the room.

She said, "Dear, there is no need to go meet your husband. He has just passed away."

In that second, the entire world blacked out in front of her. The young lady murmured, "Mother ... it is not funny. I just talked to him last night and my boy is just a baby. He hasn't had a chance to say 'daddy.' How can he grow up without a father?"

Her little boy was only a few days away from celebrating his first birthday with his father. Though not being able to speak yet, he understood. He heard that his beloved father had passed away. He stretched his tiny body as high as he could, standing for the first time, to hold his mother in his arms. And when she sank to the floor, the little boy held her face with his two hands and used his tiny fingers to gently wipe away her tears ... just as she had always done for him.

The way her little boy stood up for her made her realize that when we mature adults face challenges, we uselessly keep asking the world for an answer, just like banging our head against the wall again and again, asking, *Why has this happened to me?* We are so self-centered that we just let ourselves drown in sorrow, forgetting that seeing us in pain hurts our loved ones even more.

She thought in wonder at how the little boy did not care for himself but only to how to make his mother feel better, and it immediately struck her that she must live. Not merely live, but live as best as she possibly could for herself and her little man.

But life is not always so simple. At the funeral, on the morning of New Year's Day, her husband's bank creditors and shareholders came calling for their shares. She learned then she had inherited $3 million in debt.

I, Me, Mine is Suffering

Hearing the story, we may feel some sympathy for her. However, if that was our business that just collapsed, our money that vanished overnight, our spouse that suddenly died, our child wiping our tears—if it were ours instead of hers, if it were us instead of them—would we merely feel "some sympathy"?

Unfortunately, that woman was me. The business that collapsed was my business, and the man who died in the story was my husband.

That little boy was my son, wiping my tears.

At the funeral, an old man walked up and told me a story.

"In the time of the Buddha, the Enlightened One, a mother who lost her child carried his tiny body, crying out for someone to bring back his life.

She went to beg the Enlightened One for her child's life back. He told her, "If you can find lettuce seeds from a home where no one has ever lost a loved one, I will help you."

"Delightedly, she ran up to every house. Everyone was willing to give the lettuce seeds to help save her son.

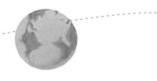

But when she asked if they had ever lost their loved ones, everyone said yes. Some had lost their parents. Some had lost their spouses. For others, they had lost their relatives, or their siblings, or their children. There were no families that had never suffered the loss of a loved one."

The trouble with using experience as a teacher is that the final exam often comes first and the lesson second.

Anonymous

Every family has lost their loved ones.

On hearing this story, I was awakened. Sadness disappeared. Light shone through my mind.

Awakened like someone who had been blind and now saw sunlight for the first time. Like someone who had always lived in a dark cave and came out to the light for the first time.

There is a word, just one word, which is powerful enough to create tremendous suffering. A word that strikes to the very core of our hearts ... that word is 'mine'.

I, Me, Mine

Everyone alive has lost someone, or something, that was a part of his or her being. But when it's someone else who loses that something or someone, when it's someone else who is in distress, we may feel some sympathy but we don't feel any suffering at all. What belongs to others—if it dies, goes bankrupt, or disappears—it doesn't matter, as long as it's not mine, not ours. Suffering comes when we feel, *This is mine. This is a part of me. I want it to be this way with me forever.*

See how our mind reaches out like energy waves and tie ourselves to our belongings, wanting them to be just as we want them to be. When they are not, we suffer.

Our mind reaches out to grasp our possessions, but it's like a hand grasping a thorn. The thorn hurts us every time we grab it, but we never learn to let go. We feel that people and things that belong to us must be the way we want them to be. When they are not, we feel the pain. Instead of coming to our senses and loosening our grasp on the painful thorn, we try very hard to change a thorn to a rose.

When you ask for light, light comes. Looking for answers, advice came to me. "If you don't want to be bankrupt, take time to examine yourself. Watch how pain rises and fades away. When you know how it works inside, you can make it work outside too. Go and be still, observe yourself in meditation."

THE KNIFE

I thought I could do that—just observe my thoughts and feelings ... observe myself ... sense my bodily movement as well as movement within my mind.

At a meditation retreat, we practiced observing ourselves through every step of our day; standing, walking, sitting, lying down, eating, drinking, thinking, and meditating.

But it wasn't easy. My mind kept reaching out; thoughts jumped here and there, losing track of the body and mind movements. The faces of the people who took advantage of my family's financial problem were right in front of me. Instead of focusing on the movement of my feet as they stepped forward, my mind was occupied with invoking terrible curses on those people—imagining that the practice of meditation could make my curse on them come true. With that thought, a smile stretched across my face.

An instructor noticed. She came and whispered to me,

"When you are in the now, every-thing comes to an end, one moment at a time ... one moment at a time."

I continued walking and that instant the wisdom light shone through my mind.

The moment my foot was about to touch the ground, my mind flashed to the person who took our company. At once, my awareness caught that thought, and when you catch your mind wandering, it stops. The picture of those people and what they did just disappeared.

I then knew that everything had passed! The things that have happened in our lives, the joys and the sorrows, the pain and the pleasure, people who said bad things and did bad things to us—they all occurred and ended, a long time ago! But I myself right then and there would not let them end. I would not lay them down or let them go. In my thoughts, I was bringing terrible scenes back to life again and again. Inside my head, everything came alive again.

The Compass of NOW

Have you ever stabbed yourself with bad thoughts? Is it time to put your knife down?

Words that cut through our heart and actions that caused us pain ended a long time ago. But we, nonetheless, relive and re-experience those words, actions, and situations, weeks, months, and even years later.

It's as if someone has stabbed us once, or more accurately, has placed beside us a knife of their unkind words and actions. Then we help them hurt ourselves, by causing our own pain.

Driving their words to pierce our heart through our thoughts again and again.

We help them succeed in putting us in pain. No one can actually cause us pain. They can create the situations, but the pain, the suffering inside, we accomplish it on our own.

It is we alone who are capable of doing it. We bring the pain to our heart by bringing the thoughts to our mind.

In our thoughts, we grab that knife and continually stab ourselves with those words and actions.

When we live in the now, we observe ourselves in this present moment, and we may think about the past or the future but the difference is that we acknowledge that we are thinking. We see how we pick up a knife of a painful thought and thrust it deep into our being. Other people may stab us once, but we stab ourselves again and again. Our suffering begins in our own mind and we can end it here, too.

Of course we'll find it is not easy to control ourselves and to stop the habit of picking up hurtful thoughts and memories that pierce our well-being.

If we cannot even control ourselves to do and be how we want, how do we expect to control others to do, say, and be the way we want them to be?

We hope for others to respond in a certain way, or for events to happen as we'd like, but how could that be possible if we can't even control ourselves?

People will do things the way they want to do them. We just don't have to let them succeed in making us unhappy.

I put my knife down.

HAPPINESS FROM FREEDOM

Nothing in life is to be feared: it is only to be understood.

Marie Curie

Twenty minutes of sitting meditation, observing our own thoughts and body can practically kill you. I felt more pain in my legs than I had ever experienced in my whole life.

The instructor said, "Observe your pain. Face your pain. Wherever the pain goes, your awareness follows."

As I sat and observed myself, I realized that my pain throbbed quickly, like a flashing lightbulb that seems constant but is actually blinking on and off very quickly.

In that moment, truth manifested. The killing pain separated from me. My observation became awareness. The pain that flashed on and off became separate from me, as if the pain belonged to someone else.

In that present moment, there wasn't even me. Therefore, there was no suffering. There was only the flow of observation. It was beautiful and not troubling at all.

When our mind observes with equanimity, our concentration and awareness are firmly rooted, so there can be no agitation. The suffering and pain stay where they are, where they came from, and no longer pierce through our heart. Just being there, separately.

If the pain that feels so real in our body can be observed as if it belongs to someone else, it does not agitate us. Everything in our mind can be observed and separated, and then it no longer causes agitation.

From that day on, I saw that my debts were just debts and nothing else. They existed on their own, separate from my mind. That problem is just a problem and nothing else. It exists on its own, separate from my mind. My mind is my mind and nothing else. It exists on its own, separate from external influences.

In that moment of knowing, a ray of happiness beamed through my heart. I tasted, heard, and felt freedom—the ultimate freedom for mankind, unlike any other freedom. True freedom, like none I imagined before.

This Too Shall Pass

If you don't have debts, you may not understand. Those of us who have debts tend to think that once our debts are paid off, we would be happy again.

But in that moment of knowing, even with all my debts and the pains in my legs, I was happy in that present moment. It was a wonderful moment of happiness. I knew I could exist side by side with my debts and my pains, co-existing happily and separately.

In that moment of existing separately, side by side, with no agitation, suddenly the pain disappeared.

I felt the moment of lightning, the moment of brightness, the moment where one is all and all is one, no inside, no outside. Just being.

I saw how it happened when you don't put your energy towards something—no pushing out, no pulling in—it vanishes from your life. Things rise and pass away on their own anyway, but our in-equilibrium energy towards them makes them go in the opposite direction of our wish.

When you don't spend energy to push away anything you don't like, it disappears on its own faster than when you do.

From this experience, I have gained the most valuable insight. Every single thing in our life, in this universe, reaches a time it must come to an end, or pass on to another condition or state.

The Compass of NOW

Whenever you suffer, see how your mind feels—heavy, shrinks, or gloomy. Look inward to see what your mind wants that conflicts with the nature.

Everything must change, whether it be the life of someone we love, the status of a relationship, a particular problem we're facing, or a physical pain.

We've all experienced hopelessness at times when we felt our problems and sufferings would never cease. When we're twisted with suffering, we want so badly for the pain to go away and it doesn't. But when we accept the pain and don't use our energy to push it away, when we coexist side by side with it, it does leave—on its own, completely.

What made us suffer wasn't the throbbing pain in our legs, it was our mind wanting the pain to go away immediately, wanting things to be how we want them to be, right here and right now.

My debts themselves did not cause me to suffer. When our loans were approved, we were excited. But then having to pay back those loans, I suffered, because I wanted that problem to vanish immediately.

The desire to have things the way we want causes us great suffering and does not help make things better.

Come to think of it, as long as we are still humans, there will always be something for us to handle. What the natural world demonstrates clearly is that everything begins and ends, rises and declines, appears and disappears ... everything changes. Nothing remains fixed in one state or condition forever. We are not capable of forcing anything in nature to stay the same just because it suits us. Nature is forever in-flux—moving, shifting, turning, accelerating, slowing down, rising, falling ... ever-changing.

We suffer when our mind stretches forth to seize hold of something, or someone, and make the impossible claim, *This is mine, this is a part of me. This thing or this person must be the way I want it or him to be, and it must always be like this.*

There is nothing permanent except change.

Heraclitus

A Fistful of Thorns

Have you ever observed that when we suffer, we usually feel that the suffering is overwhelming? And we have no idea how to stop it. It doesn't matter how small the problem is. Even just being gossiped about can sometimes cause over-whelming suffering.

Picture this: Your mind is a hand and your painful thoughts are thorns. Your mind unthinkingly squeezes these thorns tightly and holds them in its grip, over and over, for long periods of time. Immense pain and suffering result and you cannot let go.

By practicing self-awareness, we can sense our mind re-lentlessly tightening its grip around distressing thoughts and thereby intensifying our pain and suffering. In that moment we can sense our mind squeezing the thorns, stabbing us with that knife. That's the very moment the mind is able to release its grasp of those thoughts, to lay down that knife.

We might be able to lay aside our suffering for a moment at this point, but then it would come back. Have you ever heard the story of the monkey who hated shrimp paste?

Shrimp Paste and The Monkey

In Asia, monkeys tend to steal food from people's homes. To put them off, people spread shrimp paste on the monkeys' hands. Monkeys loathe shrimp paste. They would first sniff it, then furiously rub and scrape it off with whatever's around, until their hands openly bleed. What is it that causes the monkeys to seriously injure themselves like this — the shrimp paste itself, or the revulsion for shrimp paste in the monkey's mind?

Monkeys do not practice self-awareness. They, therefore, do not know that the more they hate the shrimp paste, the more they would sniff it, for which increases the ensuing disgust and the obsession to wipe it off. They are responsible for the critical damage they do to themselves.

Some of us might laugh and ridicule the monkey for being so ignorant. But every one of us has been this monkey. The more we despise something, the more we bring it close to our heart. We do this without being aware.

Are we humans going to let ourselves be like the monkey with the shrimp paste?

Will we allow those who want to harm us to be successful in causing us pain? And not just us, we also invite them to harm our loved ones as we bring our sorrow home.

When will we say enough is enough?

Inner Laboratory

Most of us think we have been awake in our life. But the truth is, all along we have been asleep even with our eyes open. Like people fully submerged in water, we are drawn by the strong currents of moods, thoughts, and feelings that mercilessly engulfed our minds and caused us great pain.

It might be strange coming to this realization—it's almost as if we were never really living our life. Our overburdened mind mindlessly led us. We lived only in our thoughts—thinking about our children, our work, our past, our future but never really being present. We never live in the present moment. We are consumed by thoughts. We are lost in our own mind, tied up in it, and do not know how to set ourselves free.

When we miss the present moment right in front of us, we miss our appointment with our life. We miss seeing our children grow up. We miss their laughter. We miss the senses, the feel, the touch of our loved ones because we are consumed by our thoughts. Only our thoughts seem real.

When we train ourselves anew to walk, eat, and speak with self-awareness, we also monitor any movement within our mind. When we do, our feelings will become as clear as day to us. We become like another person watching ourselves, but one who has the right to choose to act in accordance with a certain thought—or not. We transform into someone who is genuinely free: because we can override our thoughts and feelings.

We rely on our minds to think, to be creative with our work, to be passionate, to love, to understand, to be happy. Our mind practically does all the important things in life for us. Actually, to be successful and joyful, we do that through our mind. And yet we know so little of how our mind works and how to take care of it to achieve the most from our life. We spend more time on less important things because we do not know that we can just look into our heart and face the emotions; for example, acknowledge and observe our fear and fear will subside.

When we are mindful, we become like a scientist in our own personal laboratory. Our body and our mind are our objects of study. At this moment, if you observe your inner workings, you'll sense your mind stretching forth to engage with the letters on this page. It reads and interprets, stops to ponder over the meaning for a bit, wanders over to other matters, then snaps back to return to reading this page. Our thoughts are innumerable, our thought paths are endlessly winding, ever-flowing and intertwining—we hardly keep up with them.

It's not surprising then to realize that our thoughts have repeatedly led us to do things that inevitably lead to sorrow, pain, and misery. We just never catch these thoughts in time, again and again.

Let's imagine ourselves as detectives, trailing wrongdoers. We catch thoughts as soon as they arise, inspect them, and if they're not harmful, we let them continue their course. Many people might feel that they have their own mind well under control, but if they think back carefully, they'll see that quite often they've let themselves be overtaken by hurtful feelings—anger, jealousy, envy, stress, anxiety, or despair. We clamp doggedly onto these feelings; even though we know very well that they have never benefitted anybody in any way.

To summarize, our mind works 24/7 to both harmful and beneficial ends. It is a heavy mental and emotional burden we always carry—a tremendous weight we bear without ever being fully aware of it.

We do not have to surrender to our moods, thoughts, feelings, or memories. Whatever rises up within us will rise up whether we like it or not, but we have the ability to simply observe them and let thoughts and feelings pass away, like watching snakes passing by without letting them hurt us. We can acknowledge but not comply with or be consumed by thoughts. Understanding the basic laws and truths that things arise and pass away moment by moment and that we are free by just being an observer, is necessary for us to successfully lighten our mind's burden.

Taking conscious observation of our mind is the beginning of freedom for ourselves and for our mind.

We all have the right to be free. Our feelings and emotions are our choices. When we realize this, we will be free from circumstances and, even better, we are free from memories, moods, and feelings of our own.

The Compass of NOW

As you move through your daily routines, come back to observe your mind, how it is feeling, how it moves, how it reaches out and lets go, how thoughts and emotions rise and disappear.

Part 3

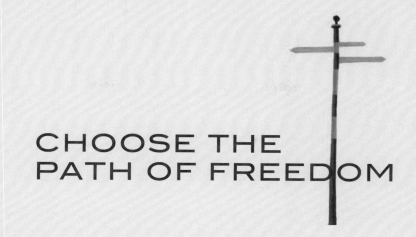

CHOOSE THE
PATH OF FREEDOM

Everything in this world is passing away. Changes, in themselves, do not cause the suffering we feel—our mind causes our suffering. Suffering arises the moment we forget to be aware of what our mind is doing in the present moment.

This is mine. This is a part of me, we think. We set ourselves on them being as we want them to be ... "I don't want her to die." "My business must always prosper." "I want him to love me forever." ... When we set our desires in this way, anguish is sure to follow.

Venerable Ajarn Chaa, a highly respected Buddhist monk, once said during one of his sermons, "A chicken is a chicken. A duck is a duck. When we want a chicken to be a duck, a chicken cannot become a duck. We strive to buck the laws of nature—that's the source of our suffering.

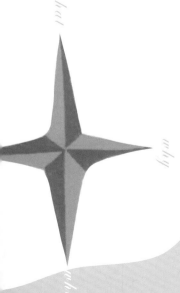

Pick up a stick—is it long or is it short? If we seek a long stick, it's too short. If we seek a short stick, it's too long. That stick is the way it is. It is our own mind that keeps us trying to control the way things are."

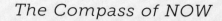

The Compass of NOW

We don't always get what we want, but we can always realize when our mind reaching out grasping and forcing things. Realizing what our mind is doing sets us light and free to deal with things happily, no matter what.

We can do our best in all situations. We can also keep our mind free. When our mind reaches out and forces itself on things, our desire goes against the law of nature and our suffering begins.

When we expect something or someone to be in a certain way, right then and there heaviness is felt upon our mind. Upon realization of what we are doing now, our mind is letting go. For a moment, we are free. Realization of now is the essence of happiness. We cannot always have everything the way we want, every time we want it. But we can always be happy and free when we know the NOW. The choice is entirely upon us.

Our Mindfulness is our Compass

Awareness is our life compass. It tells us what we are really doing, where this action or feeling is taking us—Do we want it? If not, then we let go, noticing moment by moment, when our mind attaches to something. We can have goals and purposes. And we can achieve our goal with our mind free, independent, happy, and serene. In each action and step we take and make when we are fully in the now, we are complete. The journey becomes the destination. Happiness is right here and now. The path gives us as much satisfaction as the goal.

Our mindfulness is the compass, by which each of us may direct the course of our life. Self-awareness can be practiced anywhere and anytime. Once our mind latches onto a mood, it becomes heavier with thoughts and emotions. By developing self-awareness, an awareness separate from our burdened mind, we can sense the mind working. We can become aware of the knife being grasped, the thorn being clenched, the shrimp paste being sniffed— it's in this initial moment of inner vision that our intense grip on that thought or mood is relaxed—and we begin to breathe more fully.

Feeling sensation within our mind the moment it begins, the very moment a particular thought, desire, or mood is taking shape—here we are seeing the very origin of a suffering-to-be. At the same time, this can be a moment that dissolves that suffering-to-be. The cause of our suffering is a mind that has lost track of itself, that continues on, impulsively, blindly, following patterns built up unconsciously over years. The moment we sense our mind drifting in a negative direction, our suffering stops. Our mind will not drift during that moment of noticing. What we have in that moment is pure self-awareness. We truly be ourselves.

We must accept the essential reality that nothing remains unchanged. We cannot order and arrange our world the way we want it to be. When we ease our grip on such impossible urges, our suffering eases. We then arrive at the most refined state of being: no person, no thing, and no event can wrench us back into the fog of agitation, anxiety, and suffering. We are composed and serene. Hurtful feelings arise only when we lose track of ourselves.

Each moment we carry on our life with full self-awareness, it means we're doing everything to the best of our ability. We have created freedom from fears, from desires. We don't have to wait for our life to be good, the goodness begins now and continues into the future.

Know Fear is No Fear

Whether we realize it or not, we have fears emerging in our mind. We fear falling into poverty, we fear people not liking us, we fear rejection, we fear that the future will not turn out as we hope, or as we expect. Or we might regret the past, how it could have been, or should have been. Stress, arising from such worries, wears down our body and mind.

Look into our heart eye-to-eye with our fear. Sensing fear the moment it appears, we see there is nothing in fear to be fearful of. Fear is just the sensation of our heart shrinking. And as we see it, the fear disappears and the heart blooms.

By learning to sense the fear the moment it arises, it becomes just a sensation and we experience greater stability and strength. Once our life experiences a deep, stable calm. We will see the freedom. We will truly realize for ourselves that we are able to achieve happiness—from within. It is happiness that does not depend on another person, or on a thing. It is an inner freedom that we can feel at any time.

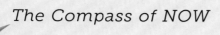

The Compass of NOW

Check into your mind. Are you tolerating some unhealthy issues in your good life? What are your fears? By being in fear, we get what we are fearful of immediately.

At this moment, you, the reader, are aware that you're concentrating on the words of this book and your mind feels stable—then it may stray elsewhere, losing its sense of itself, as you perhaps daydream for a few seconds, or maybe minutes—and then back to focus on the words of this book, resuming your self-awareness.

Tail-ache

At the meditation retreat, we had the task of observing our body and mind. One man got up from his sitting meditation and said, "If I stay in this position any longer, I'll become paralyzed because I'm aching all over—my head, my neck, my back, my legs, and my whole body."

A granny immediately joined in, "That's right. I sit on a chair, and I can't sit for another five minutes before my bones would feel like they could snap into little pieces. It's strange. When I sat at home playing cards non-stop for three days and nights, my grandchildren would bring me food and drink while I was playing. Then I could sit just fine—no problem, no pain!"

Someone turned towards the man and asked, "Are you in pain all over your body? Including your tail?"

The man replied, "No."

She then told him, "Uhhh, it's good you don't have a tail. Because if you did, I'm sure your tail would be hurting as well,."

Some may find this amusing, but if you really think about it, it is not amusing at all. If we had a tail, the tail would probably be yet another source of suffering in our life—because we would make it so. Everything we have, everything that we are a part of, we worry about it. The more we have, the more we worry. The more we don't have, the more we worry, too.

And what must we do? Should we give up all that we have, all that we are a part of, in order to end this suffering; end all our problems? No. The truth is that we can keep everything and also keep our heart independently serene. It's all about monitoring our mind. Whenever our mind attaches itself to something or someone, or wants things to be a certain way, we must make ourselves aware of this at once. The moment we sense our mind attaches to thoughts and desires, that moment we let go.

We love ourselves and want to avoid pain. If we accidentally pick up something that's burning hot, we would drop it immediately. If we actually sense the suffering inside of ourselves, we can drop that too. Observing our mind helps separate us from our own moods, feelings and pain. Awareness enables us to stand apart and see how the feeling happens and vanishes. It enables us to be free.

Being mindful does not mean we might lose the intensity or determination in our life. A sprinter who carries a heavily burdened mind—how can he compete with a sprinter who has no such burden? We can have a meaningful life filled with purposes and goals without fears and pressures on ourselves.

Feces Worms

Nowadays many people think they know everything, believing that they have happiness in their lives, though unaware of the true life purpose of mind development, They run through life like they are in a rat race, like pigs being raised and fattened for an eventual slaughter. We take in petty enjoyments and are lured in deeper and deeper. We have taken the bait and become hooked. The hook remains embedded in us and generates profound pain and suffering. There is a way to unhook ourselves, to free our mind.

One forest monk in Thailand put it this way: we are like those tiny worms that infest a pile of feces. If we moved one worm away from the reeking pile, what would the worm do? It would strike out immediately, headed back towards that pile of feces.

This is like the times in our life when we had the chance to extract ourselves from harmful people, habits, or lifestyles, but we let ourselves slide back into those harmful habits or circumstances, simply because we were used to them— even if they were rancid and foul-smelling.

It takes strength and determination to train us. Nothing in life worth having comes easily. A university degree can take

many years to acquire. But how many of us do make a serious effort to acquire the expertise in the knowledge of our inner self? Some never take the time to investigate their own mind and rather put their energy and focus in other people and external things. How many of us give ourselves just a few days, away from the routine of our lives, to seriously investigate our mental and emotional workings—and finally know ourselves?

THE CAUSE OF THE PROBLEM

Many of us may think that external things—work, money, people, etc.—are what created all our problems. But when we look into ourselves, the cause of our problem actually originates inside us—inside our very own body and mind. The good news is if it starts inside, we can end it here.

No matter how well we take care of our body, there are still pain and deterioration. When we have pain in our body, we normally have to rely on pain medications to stop us from feeling it. In addition, the pain in our body will be increased with the pain in our mind, wanting the body's pain to go away. So we not only have the body pain, but we also have the emotional suffering, and

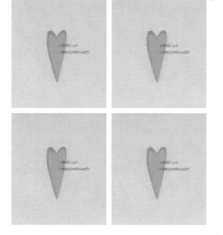

our suffering can leak out to hurt or harm our loved ones who are around us too.

By practicing observing our body, breathing, and mind movement, our mind gains strength and wisdom. We can see that the body pain is just some pulsing heat, and our mind is independent from the body pain. This is possible if we become aware and stop adding our hatred of pain or the feeling of wanting the pain to go away, which only magnifies it. We can even objectively look at things that normally hurt us: debts, bad relationship, defamation, gossip, work stress, financial challenges. Seeing the feeling as it is, we can recognize that the feeling is only some moving sensation. The fear and anxiety that occur are the results of our mind stretching out with desires and grasping the situation with attachment. Our happiness insurance tool is that no matter what feelings arise, we can just observe them. The faster we see them, the sooner we let them go, and the sooner we will be free. When we notice the feelings objectively, they cannot hurt us or make us do things that we might regret. We begin to live our life by conscious choices. We let go of our own harmful feelings. When we train ourselves to be conscious, that gives us ultimate freedom and happiness insurance. The choices we make in life nourish our well-being, internally and externally.

This is the ultimate knowledge for mankind.

CRAVING

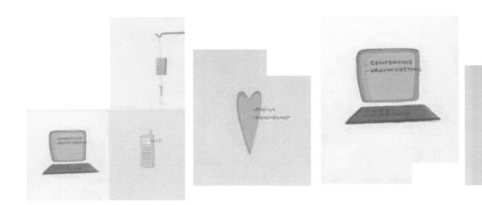

Have you ever had a craving for a particular something to eat: a craving so clear, so strong, and so undeniable that nothing can stop it? That desire even just for a bar of chocolate must be fulfilled someway, somehow. Our desires and thoughts lead us down a path, and we unblinkingly run headfirst after them. Where's it leading? Do we even want to be on this path? Where does it take us? Let's say it's not about a bowl of noodles but about larger cravings—like falling for a married person. Or perhaps it's the desire to have luxurious houses and cars that are out of reach. If we don't watch carefully over our mind, we could begin weaving a web of emotional torment that will ensnare ourselves and other people. Such yearnings lead us to take foolish risks. We may find ourselves deceiving others to get what we want, or to "be" what we want to be. We may "reason" with ourselves, I'm really in love with him. It's my right. I deserve him as much as she does, even more than she does.

We train pet dogs and cats to go to the bathroom and to be obedient in general. A new employee gets training for the job he's undertaken. But our very own self-awareness, by which our life is led, has never had any training! We let our mind roam free like a puppy without any caretaker. When we want to do something, we just go ahead and do it. But when suffering the result—we're powerless against it.

Cars need to have brakes so we can stop them whenever and wherever we need to. Houses need to have fences. But our mind works without a brake to slow it. Vigilantly watching over ourselves—this is the brake and the fence each mind needs.

The Big Glass

We've all been told to look for the positive side in every-thing, like that glass of water—it's half full, not half empty. Whichever way we view it, however, we'll still see it as something is missing.

Maybe the glass is too big. If we choose the glass size to match our water, then our glass is always full, adequate, and easy to drink from. Or we can choose even a smaller glass and have more water than we need, enough and plenty to share.

The glass is like our desires and water is the things we have. Human desires, if not being watched, will continue to grow no matter how much one has, and happiness will always elude us. Happiness is not about what one has but about what one appreciates. When our mind stops search-ing and starts breathing in the fresh air of awareness, we start to be fulfilled.

All we need to do is to be aware of our desire once it arises and sends sensations around our mind and body. Observing those urges and impulses, takes our mind off the objects or people, and back to ourselves, our breathing, and we become free from being the slave of our emotions and desires that keep dragging us up and down in life.

The Compass of NOW

How many times a day do you catch your wants and desires? The moment you notice them, see how your desires shrink. Resize your desire-glass and be happy with what you have now.

When our glasses are the size of what we already have, some may wonder if we will still be successful and happy. Certainly, we can still put immense effort and will into our pursuit of wealth and happiness that are in line with our life's purposes and values and into finding more water to put into our glasses, but our attitudes will be different. We do our best and enjoy and learn from our results no matter what. The secret of happiness is that we resize the glass to match the amount of water we now have, to be content with what we have and enjoy it today. Appreciation brings more joy and more of what we appreciate. We train ourselves to be able to be happy. Happiness needs the ability to be happy. If one does not know how to be happy with $100, don't wish that $10 million will bring happiness, or will arrive. Happiness and contentment, in and of themselves, bring sustainable wealth and happiness. Without contentment that comes from the understanding of life's truth, one cannot succeed or the success will not be sustainable. We can't wait for the contentment to come. We can be content at this moment— right now.

At the time I inherited $3 million debt, sitting in our garden under the tree with my sister, I told her that I felt happiness and that life was beautiful. My sister exclaimed, "You have lost your husband, your son has no father, bankers are chasing after you, and you say life is beautiful?" Smiling at her, I replied, "Yes." That peace, contentment, and serenity took me through everything. I paid off all my debts, and made enough wealth to be financially free.

With half a glass of water, if we resize the glass to one-fourth of its original size, we'll have more than what we need. We'll have plenty for ourselves and enough to share with others. When our glass is full, we won't rush. We'll always have time for our loved ones, for our kids, for our own self-enrichment—for all those things that have profound meanings to us.

The secret to this is to be happy and content with what you have. Contentment brings joy and joyful people do joyful things and bring more joy to their lives and others.

LET GO

The first time I left the meditation retreat, the Thai government floated Thai currency on the international market, resulting in Baht devaluation, triggering the 1997 Asian Financial Crisis. The Thai economy screeched to a sudden halt. The moment I received a call informing me about the news from the banker, my knees buckled and tears streamed down: How could I ever hope to pay back such an enormous debt in this situation?

The moment that thought, with its pang of suffering, jolted me, my mind immediately flashed awareness of it—and the suffering instantly subsided.

I saw the mind that dropped to my feet, but there was another mind observing. That observing mind was content, serene, and composed. That instant I knew even if I had very little left, I would still be content. Anything I achieved would be an extra success and bring extra joy. When you accept the lowest point possible and be consciously free from fear, your mind becomes big and crystal clear.

To my astonishment, this is our human ability: we can watch our mind drop and totally dissociate ourselves from it. With wise, firm dissociated mind, we become the great advisor for ourselves. We can then see things from the broadest perspective and make great decisions.

That day, I solved my debt issue like cutting out infected organs in order to save my life. Wherever it hurts, let it go. Which assets, companies, and partnerships I couldn't take care of, whatever was beyond my strength—I just let it go. In two years, I managed to pay back my entire debt. I was free and independent. I was financially free to choose my own path, where I wanted to live, with whom, and how and when I wanted to work, by keeping my glass small. What my son and I had was enough to keep our glasses always full.

At thirty-five years of age, I left the world of the diamond business and moved to a beach house to live a peaceful life with my child on a life path we have chosen for ourselves.

The best way for each of us to live our own life is to be found deep within each of us. Our body and mind constantly send signals and sensations to tell us that the things we want to do should be done or should be let go. We can practice listening deeply to ourselves with our quiet mind, which we can achieve right here and now.

The Secret of Happy Life

The quality of life begins with awareness, watching over senses that come through our eyes, ears, nose, tongue, body, and mind. We have six doors that open to the world. Our awareness is the lifeguard over these doors. We observe what comes in, how our internal system interprets it, observe the sensation that follows, and notice the feeling of wanting or pushing it away. And here we have a period of choices—the moment we make a conscious decision based on our awareness.

Imagine life without awareness. Do you want to spend your life like a fish being hooked by a bait all the time? Would you spend your whole life being a slave to your sensations, always in turmoil, grabbing to pull in what you like, and fighting to push away what you dislike? Or would you like to learn from the sensations, to be an observer of your mind, and be happy no matter what?

Humans have the ability to watch over ourselves and be free. When we can sense the feeling of sadness arising in our mind, then we are not sad. If we can see the sensation of anger occurring, then the anger cannot consume us. We can notice our desire for a handbag, but as we see it, we can rise up and see the overall picture of our life and choose to buy or not to buy with wisdom. The desire does not consume us.

The best thing about being aware is that when something not so pleasant happens to us, like losing something dear, for example, if we set one of our life's purposes as achieving inner-self development, then we would learn from all sensations and feelings—not just enjoying the pleasant ones and pushing away the unpleasant ones. When we set our life course to be on developing our understanding, then we can benefit and learn from every situation and everything can have some good sides for us.

We learn and we grow, so no matter what happens, our awareness always elevates our life to the best position.

Illusion

Before practicing to reckon what our mind is doing now, we might not know that the fire burning in our mind, which can make us become anxious, unsettled creatures, originates inside us. We might seek for the causes of our discontent in our surroundings, including in the people with whom we interacted. We looked around for ways to turn the fire down: buying things, moving things around, finding a new partner, always hoping that a deep, lasting joy would result.

Often, the things that we think will make our life easier, actually make it more difficult—unless we are practicing to reckon what our mind is seeking. We have cars to save us time getting around, but with this extra time we choose to go out more than we would otherwise, so we really end up losing time to spend with our loved ones. We expand our roadways and demolishing homes to decrease traffic congestion. Yet simultaneously, more cars are being bought and driven and traffic congestion has in no way decreased. Now how much time of our life do we spend sitting in traffic? Household laundry and dishwashing machines—do they really lessen the amount of housework we have and save us time and energy? No. Because these machines do their jobs so fast and easily, we end up carelessly using more clothes and more dishes than we have to. So it seems that we end up washing more clothes and more dishes—just because we can. Phones make it possible to communicate without traveling to see the other party. But now we chat idly on the phone, even during the time we spend with family. We have equipped our life with convenience appliances and labor-saving devices of all kinds—so why is it that we end up having less quality time to ourselves? These "time-saving" appliances and devices—without the awareness of how, why, and when to use them—they can consume our life. There is nothing in the world that can satisfy our thirst. When we know how to regulate our desires, then and only then, the contentment and tranquility are found.

The Compass of NOW

See how advertising stirs your mind to desire for some items. The moment you notice, you are the true master of your life and independently making choices that really suit you, not the advertiser.

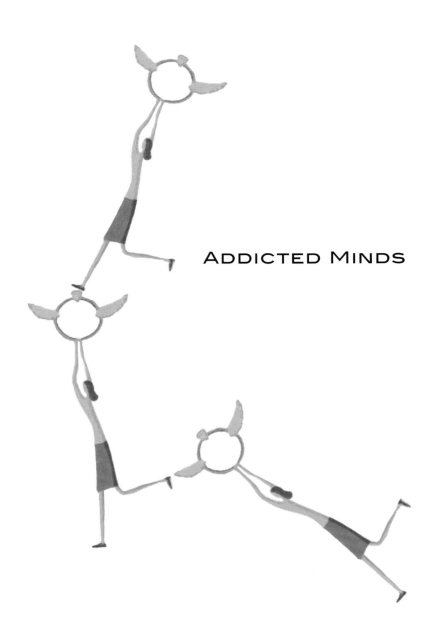

Addicted Minds

Material wealth, work, friends, and loved ones—each of these is something we can see and touch. It's not surprising then, that when we become irritated, stressed, or restless, we find ourselves seeking escape from such moods through one of these "diversions." We might become addicted to one or more of them because they take our mind away from painful thoughts and emotions; even though the relief they give is brief. The real problem, of course, is always right there with us: our unguided mind.

Solving problems by pushing them to the side and spending time on diversions is like a drug addict who flees his problems through the drug high. And so it is when we escape to our Facebook, websites, TV, shopping, pubs, bars and so on.

What is most important to know is that when we've been hooked on external factors, we'll lost our ability to feel any happiness on our own. We'll have to rely on outside elements to feel happy. Furthermore, we'll need greater and greater amounts of the same things to receive less and less satisfaction—until we look for something new. So on and on, the cycle repeats itself. We find ourselves working more to support our addictions, take more risks ... and deviate, little by little each day, from our dearest, most fundamental life purposes.

The Novice, His Robe, and The Mouse

There's a story of a novice who aimed earnestly to practice meditation. He stayed near the village by the edge of a forest. There, isolated, he could fully devote himself to deep contemplation. One day, a mouse came and nibbled on his one spare robe. The next day it came again. Rather than taking care of this problem directly by putting the robe in a place the mouse could not reach, the young novice decided to solve his problem by getting a cat around the hut to keep the mouse away. Now he needed milk to feed the cat. But he was not always willing to go down to the village to request milk, and so he resolved that problem by acquiring a cow. Now he needed to tend to the cow—but he still wanted to devote himself to his meditation practice. So he hired one of the village women to tend his cow. Eventually, his money ran out and he could no longer pay the woman. One thing led to another, so he went ahead and married her, left the monkhood, and took up the life of a farmer. So much for saving the robe.

Instead of solving the problem directly at its source—he sought elsewhere for solutions—the novice monk ended up deviating widely from his goal of earnest meditation practice. Little by little, day by day, with the deviations so small that they went by unseen ... until it was too late and his lifestyle had been transformed—and it all began with a mere mouse and a robe.

How many times in our life do we solve our problems by creating more problems, deviating further from our goals? One man felt his life was empty when he got home after work and spent his evening alone, so he got married. After a few years, love faded, so he decided to have kids to bind his family together. With three kids, he needed to buy a bigger house, a bigger car, and took a bank loan to expand his business. He worked very hard and hardly spend time with his family. Whenever they're together, they often argued. So, he tended to spend his evening alone. He felt emptier, though heavier with more debts.

There was a hardworking businessman. He had been working hard but his business hadn't done well. He had just bought an SUV, hoping to use it to take his family to the countryside. The morning he was about to take his family on vacation, the first time they would all be together for quality time, just before they were about to depart, a bank agent came to seize the car, which was in arrears. The man ran into his house, got a gun, and in front of his family, shot the agent and then himself.

Many people misdirect their attentions the moment the problem arises. They look in the wrong places to find solutions. Meanwhile, their problems keep growing in size and complexity until they've tied their lives up in knots that are impossible to work loose.

They simply miss what their minds are doing now.

It is easier to escape from the feelings that arise in us. But not facing the emptiness, anxiety, fear, guilt, and so on, can lead us to things that take us away from our chosen path. People create more problems because they do not take care of the problems at the root. The root is where the feeling arises. If you feel empty, look at your emptiness, face it. When you just look at your feeling, sense the sensation or movement in your mind, the feeling stops there. You have choices over your emotions. As you become aware more often, your awareness become stronger and more automatic. You become aware of yourself more naturally and your mind reaches another level, obtaining a pilot's view of things. A mindful life gives you happiness right here and right now. This moment of awareness fulfills you.

Content, self-fulfilled people attract fulfilled and content partners. They have respect for and faith in themselves and are ready to love, respect, and have faith in others.

Fulfilled and content hearts draw more fulfilled and content lives. Happy, meaningful deeds bring even happier and more meaningful lives. Therefore, before beginning any journey, decision, action, we should start observing our mind and get into the state we want our life to be in, right here and now.

Happiness is here and now.

THE PEANUT-MONKEY

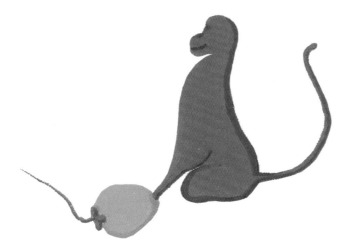

Many, especially those in the banking industry, asked me, "How did you do it—paid back all that money, with the economy as bad as it'd been?" Often I responded by relating to something I once saw on television concerning how Thai farmers catch the monkeys that eat up their crops. Monkeys are very agile creatures. But to catch one, all a farmer has to do is take a coconut, make a hole in it, and put something the monkeys love to eat, like peanuts, inside. A monkey, sensing food, will run over to the coconut, smell it, insert its hand through the hole, and grab a fistful of peanuts. When it then tries to withdraw its hand from the coconut— it can't. The farmer would then come up from behind and snare the distracted monkey.

The monkey cannot run or climb away because its hand is stuck in the coconut. We may laugh at the monkey, thinking how foolish it is. To be free, all it has to do is letting go of the peanuts, something it really likes and something that kills it. It can let go of the peanuts and be free and save its life.

We can sometimes be like the monkey, clinging stubbornly onto certain thoughts and desires, *This is mine. This must be the way I want it to be. It can only be this way.* Every suffering we have comes from holding onto our wants too stubbornly. We are just like the peanut-monkey— being too attached and consumed by our desires, clinging too much to our wants, and thinking everything must always be how we want it to be.

If that monkey had practiced any self-awareness, it would have seen that all it had to do was release its grasp. When we let go, we can see that life offers many other options. If we back up just a few steps, unlike the monkey, we'd see there are plenty of other choices. We do not have to let ourselves be locked up within our problems—if we let go, we'll see solutions.

There is nothing that causes us problems more than our own attachments. When something suddenly happens to us, we suffer because we want things to be the way we think they should be—we impossibly want the external world to conform to our inner wants and desires. Without monitoring our thoughts, we lose sight of the fact that our desires are what make us suffer. We trap ourselves.

One young lady told me she would not break up with her boyfriend; even though he brought his new woman to live in the same house, used her money, and treated her badly. She still wanted to marry him. No matter how he beat her up, broke her heart, she stayed.

Every problem has solutions. The only thing that traps us within our problem is our own need. When one holds too tightly onto something, one closes the door to opportunities and solutions. If we strongly hold onto something too much,

we would forget to think about the end results, and do not explore all of our options. We close our minds to the way out because we want to hang on to our peanuts. The difficult part is that people do not realize that their own hands are holding the peanuts.

One businesswoman told me why she didn't want to sell her land for $2 million—because she had previously had an offer of $3 million. In the end, the bank forfeited her land. She got no money out of it and still had to pay the rest of her debt to the bank. If she had not been too attached to the past opportunity, she could have sold the land, used the money to pay the bank, and still have had some money left to herself.

Her peanut was the price of the land 10 years ago.

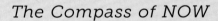

The Compass of NOW

What is your peanut?

With my enormous debt, all I had to do was to let go of the peanuts, which were the thoughts that that land, that company, that investment were ours. When I realized that, I maintained my mind and life stability despite the red figures on my bank statement. Then anything that I could manage to keep or make would be an extra gift to my life. I managed to sell everything—houses, land, diamonds, jewelry, and gold. I practically sold every piece of land we had.

Someone asked me, what is the secret to selling during the slow economy? At that time the land was worth nothing because there were hardly any transactions. People were stuck at their previous offers and did not wish to sell at lower prices. I smiled and replied, "Easy, just sell at the price buyers want to buy and you can sell anything." The listeners always exclaimed, "Sell at buyers' prices, then how can you make a profit?" My usual reply "So, do you want to make a profit, or do you want to get rid of your debt and to be financially free? If your goal is to be free from debt, then you stick to that."

People are normally swayed from their initial goals. First they want to sell their property to be free from their debt, but when buyers come along, they want to make a handsome profit

from buyers. Some people want to have a spouse as their life companion, but when they have one, they want their spouse to be their child—to obey them, and do whatever they say. Desires can do lots of things to people's lives and decisions. We must watch out for the desires that are behind our actions. Keep our eyes set on your purposes. What do we really want? What are really good for our life?

Nothing can trap us but our greed. No one can fool anyone but his or her own greed. The tighter people grasp, the more they lose. When we let go, we see the new world of abundance that begins inside us. Once we feel the abundance inside, we'll see the abundance outside.

The Compass of NOW

Life is great. Live it now.

Part 4 **FORM
PURPOSES
AND VALUES**

Setting wrong life goals can lead to wrong directions.

In ancient times in India, a young student asked his spiritual teacher. "In order to help others to the fullest of my ability, I need to be wealthy. Material needs must not limit me in my endeavor. What should I do?"

The guru responded, "In each of us, there are two goddesses. One is Wisdom, the other is Prosperity. Everybody loves and reveres both greatly. But the secret is that we must pour our greatest energy into loving and revering Wisdom. Then, Prosperity, filled with envy, will devote her attention fully upon you, almost doting upon you everywhere, all the time. When this happens, then you will have the material wealth you desire to accomplish your goals."

The Keys

Wisdom is the key that makes each human's life different from another's. Many search for prosperity their whole lives but never find it. Many have all the money but live and die as if they were poor. What is lacking for both types is wisdom.

We are all able to realize prosperity at any point in our lives. For example, a farmer walking home after a nice day in the field, stops and catches five fish. He gives two to a neighboring family and, with the rest, makes delicious curry to give alms to monks and feeds his family. Such a person has extra—he has enough and lives in abundance.

Wisdom is the understanding of the world, of nature, of humanity. If we comprehend and recognize the essential nature of money, relationships, and all aspects of living, we shall be their masters. If we don't, they shall become our masters.

Wisdom knows that nothing around us is certain and that we cannot, therefore, put our complete faith on external objects to create happiness. Happiness must be founded from within. Life that is self-aware is free, unconfused, and unagitated. It has no fears or insecurities and is able to make decisions in complete stability. The person in such a state knows how to live a life of pure quality, a life of sharing with others. He or she can become a force of positive energy attracting good things and live a life that does not have the phrase "not enough" in his or her vocabulary.

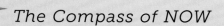

The Compass of NOW

Which Goddess are you taking care of? Remember to take care of the Wisdom before the Prosperity.

Life's Traps

There are so many things in life that are tremendously beneficial to our well-being and they cost very little, if anything: fresh vegetables and fruits, the emotional warmth of family, the enduring trust felt among old friends, the smile in our loved one's eyes, the bright rays of sunrise, and the calm hues of sunset. They all nourish our base of happiness within. Thus, it's the quality of our life without.

But there are so many things in life that are both costly and harmful, especially when we find ourselves under the sway of trends, of wanting to be a part of the local jet set, or of wanting to do or be what "everyone else" is doing or being.

When we're enjoying ourselves in damaging ways, we've fallen headlong into traps. They are traps because the enjoyment is brief but the cost—to our body, mind, and our life ... well, that is not so brief.

The best things in life are free. It's the worst things that are so expensive.

Anonymous

The Compass of NOW

What choices have you made for the purpose of superficial values that burden your life?

TRUE VALUE

Many things in life have both genuine values and artificial values, linked to consumerist social trends. The value they have for each of us depend on how we use them.

Computers, for example, are genuinely valuable to our life when used primarily to create, to learn, and to organize. But they are considered as artificially valuable when they are used only for pleasure and taking our time away from our family and things that really matter to us.

Cars can save our travelling time or make us spend more time travelling just because we have cars.

Cell phones, smart phones, iPods, electronic devices—in general, they have genuinely beneficial impacts on our well-being—unless, they are used primarily to embellish our social standing among our peers. Also, such devices often take away time better spent with our loved ones.

Awash as we are with data in this age of information and communication technology, we must, in order to benefit from it, be mindful about controlling the quantity and quality of the information that comes our way. If we accept the information without any inner process of filtration, such knowledge is like undigested food, which benefits the consumer in no way.

Before we make any decision, let us be consciously aware of the choice we are making. See what is driving us? What is the pushing force behind the decision? Where will it lead us? Practicing to detect our own tricky mind needs constant, gentle looking inward into our heart. Then to stand firm with the right choice and let go of the wrong one needs a composed mind derived from returning to our breathing, sensing our body and mind, feeling our feet touching the ground. We can smile to ourselves, enjoy this moment, this wonderful moment, and have the strength to make choices that have true values to our life and preserve the well-being of others.

Deception

One sad example: the country I come from, Thailand, not long ago, was once a land of plenty, with fish in the water and rice in the fields. Everyone was able to grow, make, find, and barter for what they needed. There was no need for money to get what was necessary. There was stability, security, and a general well-being that had been achieved over the centuries. Life's necessities were self-sustainable.

Then the so-called development spread from the West, and with it the GDP per capita was used to assess a nation's economic wealth and productivity. Thais who live in environment-friendly wooden houses amidst the vast rice fields by riverbanks—they eat freshly caught fish and naturally grown fruits and vegetables, exercise as working in their farms, and have great relationships with their neighbors through traditional ceremonies—are considered poor and economically unproductive, not contributing anything to the country's GDP because they hardly buy and sell things.

Thailand had been classified as a "developing nation" and a "Third World" country. From a largely sustainable economy, producing enough to meet our needs, we gear towards producing for exports. Our economy heavily depends on exports and foreign investment. We lost the balance of our sustainable economy. Meanwhile, our international economic status has been "upgraded" to a newly industrialized country, and yet there are more Thais living with scarcity. Economic figures are made to look promising to induce foreign investors to plunk their cash into the Thai economy—only to later take it all back with larger profits.

Development is good as long as it has a balance. Every country has its own roots and needs to be self-sufficient before it exports the excess of production, otherwise it will lose control over its well-being. A nation's future should not depend upon outsiders who can toss it around, obviously not making decisions with the nation's best interest in mind. From a nation of people with fresh vegetables and healthy diets, we have been induced to live more and more on meat and dairy products and have experienced these diets' impacts on health—obesity, heart disease, and high cholesterol—just like in the developed countries we hope to imitate.

From agricultural practices developed in harmony with nature over the centuries, we now have the Green Revolution with its rice strains engineered in laboratories. These strains must be used with costly fertilizers and pesticides because they do not have the natural immunities built up over time as those traditionally used by Thai farmers. In the long run, these newer, higher-yielding varieties have actually yielded less because the soil has been depleted of its nutrients. Moreover, the heavy use of chemicals that have leached into rivers, lakes, and ground water has caused serious environmental and human health issues.

Our fellows in the countryside, old and young, once walked with dignity and honor in their rural villages. They were also heirs to an indigenous folk knowledge and wisdom passed down over generations. Now, out of economic necessity, they have been forced to migrate into big cities, to serve as cheap labor. Many of them have been driven out of their homes by the construction of dams for electricity, so that we can stay out all night on the dance floor.

Each time we feel dissatisfied with the services we get from housekeepers, maids, drivers, cashiers, street vendors, workers, and laborers of all kinds, let's all keep in mind that it's because of our lifestyles of consumption that most of them have had to move out of their villages. They've had to leave places where they were regarded with due measures of honor and dignity, and relocate to a place where they became socially marginal. When it comes to water and electricity, we ask only: how much does it cost us? We hardly consider where the water and electricity come from. Each time we turn on the faucet or a light, consider the far-reaching impact it has had on those rural families forced off their land by the dams constructed to supply us with water and electricity. How much wildlife was drowned by its construction? How much of the environment, trees, plants, and soil were destroyed? And it's all for the sake of convenience, for luxury, for money, and for greater consumption.

When we limit our perspective to that of a consumer, we forget how our lifestyle affects others, how it affects us, and how we become more dependent on others. From the minute we wake up until bedtime, we have someone, some devices, and some social media to keep us entertained. Everything comes easily—so easily that we think very little of how things come about and how these things may affect the lives of others who have less say than we do. We become numb to lives around us and, in order to feel something, we have to buy more to hide away our deep pain, cover up the spaces in our hearts that feel empty, lonely, and lost.

In the world of marketing today, forceful advertising can influence us to consume whatever a manufacturer wants to sell. Every time we turn on the television or the radio, pick up a newspaper or magazine or browse the internet, images, text, sounds, and animations relentlessly bombard our senses. Over time, through merciless repetition, they sink into our consciousness, *I look older than I should... I could be prettier! ... Is that what people think about me? ... Do I need that plastic surgery? ... That looks like fun.* Each advertisement aims straight for the weak spots in our heart. Many create needs and wants that are harmful. Many play upon our insecurities or generate new insecurities. And many try to sell products and services we should be able to make or do on our own. So, we must jolt ourselves awake and stop them from ever luring us again.

This shallowness, lack of depth cannot be filled by best advertised items. We need to come back to our true home, our breathing, our body and mind. By coming back to our inner self, we will find depth, nourish our soul, heal wounds, and put the smiles back into our heart.

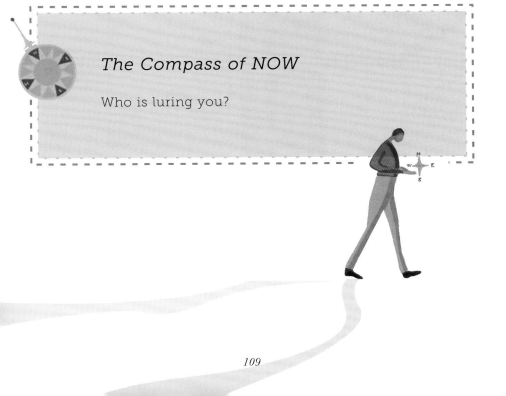

The Compass of NOW

Who is luring you?

WRONG PRIORITIES ON A NATIONAL LEVEL

Setting the wrong goals will lead our life into a whirlpool of problems with no end.

America is an example of a nation that has measured success in material terms. In doing so, it has met with astounding material success over the past century. While at the same time, there exist serious social failures paralleling with its material triumphs: from high divorce rates, broken families, health issues, mental illnesses, gun violence in schools, to a growing gap between the very rich and those at middle and lower incomes.

If a country's top priority was financial success, we might see gambling legalized to attract money into the nation. Large casinos would significantly increase the country's foreign cash reserves and create many local jobs while ruining people's lives and their families. In setting such national goals, we must realize that for every increase, there is a decrease. Are we coming out ahead at all?

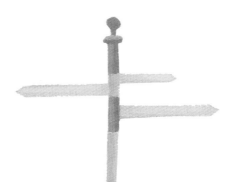

If financial statistics were a top priority of our nation, policies favoring the business sector, especially the industrial-manufacturing base, would be implemented. We would see the government making decisions tending to advance the productivity of industry at the expense of the agricultural sector. Take, for example, the construction of dams with the consequent destruction of villages, forests, and wildlife, and uprooting of people from their homes, their land, and their water supply. Consider the villages ruined for the sake of providing electricity to us. Another example is that some countries lack government regulations on how factories dispose of their chemical wastes, which result in the pollution of their water, soil, and air. Again, are we coming out ahead at all?

Another action a government that has financial status as its top priority may take is to push down interest rates on savings accounts in order to provide low-cost, start-up capital for businessmen to borrow for the purpose of opening a new business or expanding an existing one. But once all those people with savings accounts, especially those of the working class, see the drop in their yearly interest, they will feel as though they've been robbed! They've been saving money for years, for decades, to enjoy in their old age, but when the interest rates are lowered they must transfer their savings into bonds, life insurance, and stocks. The stocks rise in value and the industrial and financial sectors reap enormous profits. But when problems arise, such as country's financial crisis arise, who feels the impact of the suffering that follows?

The value of everything is expressed in financial terms; even though these numbers do not take account of all that is important. Do they really express the value? A country's GDP is a number. But what if it's the number whose value increases from the rise in sales of alcohol, cigarettes, and government lottery tickets? One bottle of whiskey may cost about as much as one hundred small cartons of milk—but this way of value comparison is false. One hundred small cartons of milk can help satisfy the hunger of one hundred children, but that one bottle of whiskey, what can it do? Can the benefit it bring match that of one hundred cartons of milk? Does the milk carry as much potential harm as the whiskey—harm to one's health, family, friends, community, and career?

There are many activities which have no economic values, but are rich in well-being values. These are activities on which we spend time and energy for the good of others without any expectation of material returns, such as volunteering, servicing community, having a happy time with family, growing vegetables in the backyard, and going for a picnic with friends. There also are the time spent in meditation and the time spent reading a book to children ... the list could go on and on. The point is that such vital activities, with their vital effects on human's well-being, are not reflected in any economic statistics, such as our per capita GDP.

When national policies do not favor certain livelihoods, such as farming, and when the crops designated for exports by the government policy are being underpriced, rural inhabitants must migrate to big cities to find work. But how much of their skills and knowledge can they use in their new occupations? They might not love their new jobs since they were never trained to work with industrial machinery.

The livelihoods of street vendors and small shopkeepers are also being squeezed out by consumerist national priorities. When roads have been widened, there are no longer any spaces for people to park their cars—to stop and buy something from street vendors. This has squelched their businesses. People now head to chain superstores with their massive parking lots, which are located on the very same roads. What will happen to the street vendors and the small family-owned shops?

Wrong Priorities at The Corporate Level

Businesses that set rapid profit growth as their one and only priority reap what they sow.

- Employees work hard, in ruthless competition against each other. Those in the senior positions also compete against each other in pursuit of power. The infighting at all levels poisons the atmosphere, crippling the business's work efficiency.
- Such businesses become cutthroat in their dealings with other businesses and lose all sensitivity of the man on the street.
- Employees have no loyalty to such firms. Corruption takes root within the firm. Employees just work the minimum each day, waiting for 5:00 p.m. to arrive.
- The business owners exploit their employees. Employees do not identify with such companies. There is neither any sense of responsibility to help the company save money, nor any desire to harness creative energy for the good of the business. Team morale becomes artificial, if it does not totally disappear.

When placing the accumulation of profits as their driving force, such businesses do not realize the high returns on a long-lasting, stable basis. They are actually harming themselves on a continuing basis.

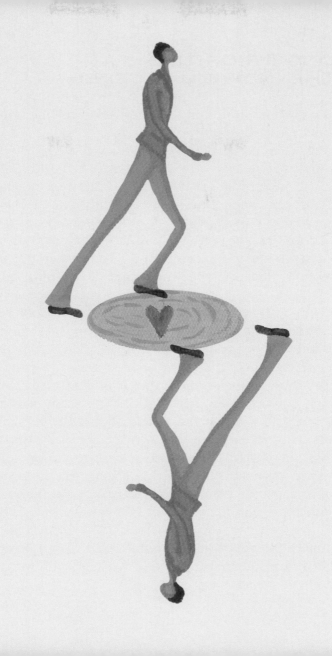

Wrong Priorities
at The Individual Level

If money is the top priority in our life, there will be nothing but troubles and disappointments ahead.

If we want to have sustainable wealth, we must be our money's master. We must know it well, use it, and not allow it to overwhelm us. Those who let money be their master will never be happy. They dread their money disappearing, and when it does, their suffering is intense. There are two sides to all things in life, including the money. What important is to know both sides—the beneficial and the harmful ones.

There's the story of an old coffee vendor who sold coffee from his small boat to customers living alongside the canal by the famous "floating market" just outside Bangkok. By noontime, when his supply all sold and the sun's rays at their strongest, the coffee vendor would relax and play his flute under the cool shade of his boat drifting softly along the river. His music warmed the hearts of passersby. This had been his daily routine for years. A tourist observing him resting in his shaded boat asked, "Old man, you've sold all your coffee. Why don't you bring more to sell, make more money, and maybe one day open up a coffee shop, and expand it into a franchise with branches all over Asia?"

"Open up coffee shops all over Asia? Why would I want to do that?", the vendor asked.

"Why? What do you mean? So you can be rich and live a good life! You can enjoy yourself, playing flute and drift along the most beautiful canals in the world.", answered the tourist.

The coffee vendor shook his head and gently paddled away. "And what do you think I'm doing right now?"

Everybody's life requirement is different. Some may be better off with their business branches all over the world— spreading happiness more widely with their services, while others may be better off with what they can handle alone. But whatever we choose to do, we must make sure we have time to nourish our heart before, during, and after our accomplishment.

A person's life consists not of what he has but of what he is.

Anonymous

Money—A Good Servant, But A Terrible Master

The wise men, when prospering, use their wealth to support development of themselves and others internally and externally, and when suffering, use their suffering to sharpen their wisdom further. While the unwise people become absorbed in money and pleasure, and lead themselves into self-set traps. We like money, we like spending it, and we like the convenience it brings to our life. Yet we must be aware that it does not end there. If we wrongly believe that *Money is my ultimate goal,* then we undermine our well-being with misunderstanding.

If money and material wealth are our ultimate goal, our decisions, actions, words, and relationships will all be directed towards achieving this goal. Our physical and mental energy and our intelligence become devoted to the pursuit of wealth. And what would happen to our life's other values, such as inner self-development, looking after family and friends, or cultivating loving relationships? We would pour our best energy into work and leave no time for our own and our family's physical, emotional, and mental health. We would frequently find ourselves at odds with others and become a large glass of water, which can be easily toppled. The physical, emotional, and mental burdens we have gathered would overwhelm us. Increasingly, we see actions other people take as being done to breach our territory. We would become too sensitive. Our desire will overwhelm and master us.

Our life has several values that are important to us. Wealth is merely one of them. So, focusing our life around money, neglecting other elements, is a mistake. For example, when the IMF was allowed to intervene with the management of the Bank of Thailand, it imposed tight controls on Thailand's financial institutions and on the government's monetary and fiscal policies, resulting in mass bankruptcy and massive break up of families. The policies focused solely on the financial interest of some, but not on the social results of these policies on the people of Thailand as a whole.

A man approached me at the end of one of my lectures. He related to me how he had once been a prosperous businessman, enjoying life with his two children and expectant wife. Then, his business encountered a serious problem and was forced to close down. He was so miserable that he couldn't see any reason for living anymore. He picked up his gun, planning to shoot his pregnant wife and their two children, and then take his own life. But his fortune intervened. The moment he was about to pull the trigger on his sleeping wife, one of his children awoke and screamed, "Dad, don't!" He froze and a thought suddenly flashed into his mind, *I thought I had lost everything. But I have my family!*

Since then he has been practicing self-awareness. Nowadays, he runs a fish ball making business, using a recipe his wife's folks had developed. Everyone in their family takes part. It's a small business, but a stable one. He no longer drives a luxury car, or lives in a mansion, but he leads a secure, comfortable, and happy life.

People who place money as their top priority often lead the lifestyles focused on building up their images as well-to-do and well-connected, successful individuals, and often harm themselves and the environment. Only the people who have meaningful life values as their top priority can truly maintain stability in life, wealth, and prosperity.

Do we have the right to use our money without any thoughts of its consequences on the lives of others and its impacts to social and ecological repercussions—locally, regionally, and globally? The widespread construction of golf courses drives up the price of land to the point that it's not worth using it for agricultural purposes. Furthermore, the pesticides sprayed to keep the golf course fresh and green drift onto surrounding fields, with local farmers reaping the ill effects. The world's billionaires take trips into space and go forward with developing a space tourism industry, while the exploitation that supports them continues, leaving the little man with no land to stand on.

A group of people, by the virtue of their accumulation of wealth through connections and dealings, seem to feel that they have the authority, the right, to harm the environment, adversely affecting the lives of children to come—but do they have this right? We live under a system in which material production and consumption are encouraged as a primary goal. People who excel at this enjoy being elevated in status, and at the same time, make far-reaching decisions based primarily on increasing material production and consumption. The human cost is overshadowed by the promise of economic gain.

In consuming the earth's resources, whether by eating them, wearing them, or using them for driving, or some other purposes—we create waste, which will be thrown away, discarded, and left behind. Not much of it is biodegradable, and it will collect upon the earth's surface and remain there for ages.

If we truly care for ourselves, care for our children and our children's children, we can expand our viewpoint beyond that of the mindless consumer. We must see our life as a part of a bigger picture and come to realize that it doesn't matter how much money we have or how much material wealth we produce. In the end, we all need the basics: fresh air, clean water, and fertile earth just as when it all began.

Live simply, so that others may simply live.
Anonymous

The Supreme Goal

Close your eyes, and visualize the life you want to have. Be aware ... observe your body and mind. Let's be consciously alert with a stilled mind—picture how you want your life to be.

Today's pace of life may often be frantic. But if you were a woodcutter and your ax had worn out so much that you found it difficult to deliver a decent result, would you go on cutting wood and keep complaining about it? If you have been working so hard that you have no time for your family or yourself, and yet the results you get are not satisfying, will you keep on working hard? Will you just put in more time and more effort when the outcome is less than satisfying?

Or will you pause to sharpen your ax?

When some choose to be ignorant, they can be unhappy before, during, and after they have chased after their own confused and mismanaged dreams. In the end, even when they have obtained their dreamed possessions, they do not know how to be happy with them and hence lose them. They are not able to keep good things for long because they don't feel they deserve them.

To make life work, we just need to add a little awareness, looking gently inward into our body and mind until it becomes automatic. Our body and mind are the two most important things that we use to create wealth, health, love, compassion, peace, and happiness. We can carry on our life as usual, but we just add our happiness insurance by

acknowledging how we feel, how our body's sensations are, and be the master of our emotions.

We can think about the past or plan for the future, but we are aware that we are now thinking. And when any emotions come in, we acknowledge them, but we do not have to accept them. We are watchful for the guests that we want to welcome into our mind.

That is the true key to happiness and success, so simple and profound: to be the master of our life, moment by moment. To be in this present moment, put a little smile on your face and joy in your heart. Enjoy this moment. This wonderful moment is truly yours.

Pursue your goals, achieve your desired outcome, do what you want to do, and enjoy every moment of knowing.

Be happy. Be successful. Be free.

Happiness Insurance

In permitting ourselves to be happy only when gaining money, acquiring new possessions, consuming certain food and drink, watching TV — the problem is that the derived happiness is limited and ultimately constrained. Once we experience financial difficulties, become ill, or age, we cannot enjoy ourselves with these external things in the way we are used to. Our suffering sharpens and our life wilts.

By adding the practice of mindfulness, we can attain our goals more efficiently. By using mindfulness to support our self-development and quality living, our life will benefit from wisdom, security, and stability. We will build up a source of happiness that is truly ours.

When we can achieve happiness on our own, free of external pressures, we will use less money. We will treat others more fairly, and will use natural resources more conscientiously. We will attain a balance in our life and have more quality time with our loved ones because we now know how to really be with them, and how to listen to and love them. Our time will be channeled into creating even greater life benefits for all.

One's outlook is a part of his virtue.

Amos Bronson Alcott

We are The World

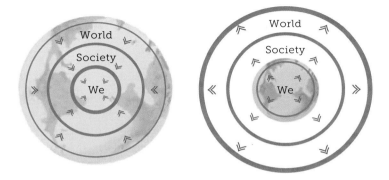

If hundreds of millions of us keep competing against one another and consuming the earth's natural resources, our communities and our planet will grow weak. Societies will compete with one another, treating each other as opponents. They vie for the earth's resources using political pressure, commercial persuasion, and military force. The planet will be squeezed, and its inhabitants will feel the increasing pressure.

Sustainable Self, Society, World

If we are self-sufficient, we are secure in our being. Even though we may not grow our own rice and vegetables and catch our own fish; we can each make a living that provides us with enough. We can stand firmly on our own feet without incurring any debt. When there is an emergency, we will have savings on hand and have mindfulness strength to tap into and get us through it. When a setback occurs, we will have faith in ourselves—faith from the good things we have done in the past and our purposeful present. When we face crises head-on with complete focus, we will be content. We will feel secure with the things we do, and be happy with ourselves and with those around us.

Our society is secure when we and those around us are secure and content—when "everyone's glass is filled". We will have free time and enough money to help others in need. Our hearts will be fulfilled as we steadily see others as our fellow humans, who have suffered as we have and upon whom we do not need to inflict any more suffering. This contentment and security trickle up, from individuals to the whole society. When we don't like somebody, we can adjust ourselves to feel as if he or she were our friend, our mother, or our child— would we wish harm to befall them then? When we have good thoughts, the positive vibes we radiate are the energy that returns to nourish our mind. When an alert mind is the root of existence—such a root carries nourishment from without that allows invigorating beauty to bloom within.

The world is secure when we are content in our life and happy among our fellow humans. We need things only as they become necessary. We consume less and throw away less. We lead the life that impacts the world adversely less and less. Fashions, which spread around the world, start from only a handful of people. Epidemics that spread around the planet start from one place with a few people. A small group of people with trained minds that shine as examples of simple, happy, prosperous living—they, too, can turn the global tide. Mahatma Gandhi, with his mental fortitude, did this, with his desire-glass so small that he required almost nothing to live contently. He, therefore, had the energy and the time to create something that has made this world a more livable place.

We make a living by what we get, but we make a life by what we give.

Winston Churchill

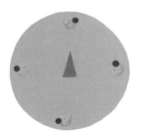

Finding Nemo in us

In the movie *Finding Nemo* (2003), Nemo, the clownfish hero of the story, is captured from the sea and put in a fish tank. His father rescues him and just as they reach the sea, a trawl net scoops him up with hundreds of other fish. All of them sink into despair and grimly accept their fate—except Nemo. Nemo exhorts all of them to flap their fins and wave their tails, to swim, swim, swim until the net breaks from the aggregate pressure of the fish. Every single one of the fish return to freedom, to their homes, and loved ones. It took only one strong heart to overturn the crisis, to overturn the current of hopelessness that had held them all.

Whenever we feel downhearted, when the world and the events around us toss us back and forth, think of Nemo—think of his strong will to be with his family, and the determination fixed upon priorities and his life path. He will never lose his way.

If we set the cultivation of understanding and stability in our mind as one of our life's top priorities, every moment of awareness is a success. Our mind grows firmer and more rooted in our well-being. Our reliance on external objects abates. Contentment is felt immediately. We have found a path on which every step of mindfulness—acknowledging our mind—brings delight in coming back to our own self, our true home of happiness. Through self-awareness, our stable mind has become like a trusted friend: ever dependable. We attain something that revolutionizes our life—spiritual independence.

Be happy with what you have and are, be generous with both, and you won't have to hunt for happiness.

William E. Gladsone

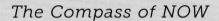

The Compass of NOW

What is your true life's purpose?

Part 5

BE TRUE
TO YOUR LIFE

My Ferrari

There was a man driving a brand-new Ferrari, zipping at high speed, when suddenly the car went out of control and crashed into the central barrier. His body was thrown out of the ripped-open car. A few moments later when he regained consciousness, he turned his head and gazed at the twisted remnant of his sports car.

In severe distress, he moaned loudly, "My Ferrari! My Ferrari!"

An elderly fruit vendor shouted back immediately, "Sir, how can you lament over your Ferrari?! Look over there! Your arm got thrown over there!"

The man turned his head and gazed at his torn, battered arm on the road. An eerie shriek came out of him, "Arghhhh!!! My Rolex! My Rolex!"

We may laugh at the story, thinking who would be more concerned with their possessions than their lives. Think again.

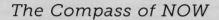

The Compass of NOW

Have you ever put so much effort into something that you overlook the things that give you joy and forget to live your life? What things are burdening you more than giving you joy?

THE HOME THAT IS ENOUGH

We will not reach the right destination by taking the wrong path. We need to take the right path. What we give importance to should be in line with our values and purposes. Our inner compass must therefore be ever-ready, alert to our thoughts, and able to detect what we are thinking and where our action will lead us to.

Most people miss opportunities to be content in their lives because of a deep misunderstanding that owning an expensive out-of-reach dream house is the only way to bring lasting happiness. Yet, we often find we must work harder in order to pay for the mortgage, to the point we don't really have the energy or time to enjoy our "dream" homes.

In a home that suits our life and our finance, we'd have money to spare, room to make choices, and our mind would be open and free for the benefits of ourselves and of others. Our money does not have to be spent on enhancing our social standing. Our life still has far to travel. So lay down those needless burdens, stop bearing those heavy weights on your shoulders—and live more fully with what you have.

Cars—The Money Drain

Many people live in unkempt rooms but drive chic cars that drain their pockets and leave no room for investment in their dreamed businesses. If they recognize the true value of cars as transportation, they would not fall into this sort of trap.

I once bought an expensive car, when I made my first million. But as I got to know and understand myself better, I asked myself how much I would be investing in this car overall, and whether it was worth it? A friend of mine had also bought a fancy European car and sold it two years later. She lost $80,000. That meant she paid $3,333 a month for the use of that car, during the two years that she owned it. We might want to do a calculation before buying a car and ask ourselves: How much of our quality time are we willing to exchange for the comfort of sitting in that car?

$$\frac{(\text{Cost of brand-new car}) - (\text{How much we sell it for later on})}{(\text{Number of years we owned the car} \times 12 \text{ months})} = \text{the ultimate cost of the car per month}$$

Are we prepared to expend our life energy, expend our hard-earned compensation for so many hours per day, just to cover the expense of that car? Thinking of it this way will make us be more cautious. *How much of my money, time, and energy will this purchase demand of me? Is it worth it?*

Whenever we make a purchase, we should consider how much of our life energy we need to expend in exchange of it. The value of our life energy per hour can be based on our per-hour pay rate from our work.

$$\text{life-energy (per hour)} = \frac{\text{Value of our labor after taxes (per day)} - \text{Value of work-related expenses (per day)*}}{\text{Amount of working hours**}}$$

If we keep a strong rein over our desires, we do not have to break ourselves working or spend too much time away from our loved ones. If we control our desires, we have the freedom to choose to do things that truly enhance the quality of our life.

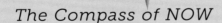

The Compass of NOW

Is the path you choose taking you to where you really want to be?

* Work-related expenses include travel, clothing, dry-cleaning, phone, meals, daycare, etc.
** Amount of hours working includes the time at work, time spent travelling to and from work, time spent buying stuff needed for work, and the time spent at work-related social affairs.

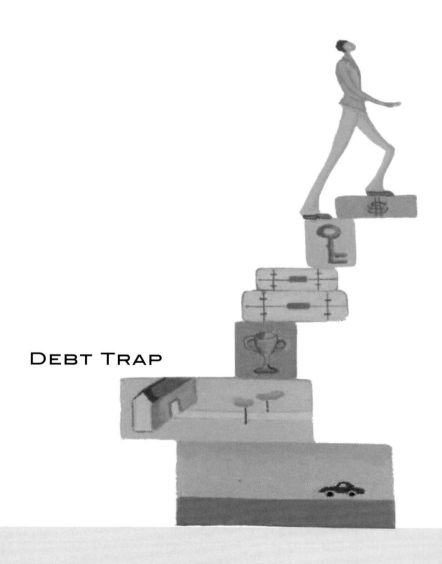

Debt Trap

People are in debt to banks and credit card companies for houses, house renovations, various appliances and accessories, electronic goods, and cars. Borrowing money means using the money we don't have at the moment, but we hope to pay it back in installments from our future earnings. Successful debt payoff depends upon a future that inevitably holds uncertainty. We may, therefore, accept more risk in our life and take higher financial risk in hope to get higher returns with which to service our debts. We may also take on work we don't want to do. Some people may even justify cheating, deceiving, or stealing from others to pay down their debts. Stress rattles them, and those around them feel it, too. People do not really understand what they're getting into when they make the decision to take on debt.

Buy and Bank are brothers. Both began working when they turned seventeen. Their parents gave them each $3,200, to use at their discretion to kick start their careers. Bank spent his sum on a small but sturdy second-hand car.

Buy used his start-up money as a down payment on a $12,000 car, borrowing $8,800 at 10% interest to be paid back in monthly installments over a five-year period. With payments of $187 per month, his debt amounted to $11,220.

Bank had no debt on his car. He decided to deposit monthly $187 into a savings fund paying 10% annual interest. After five years, his total earnings with compound interest amounted to $14,601.

He then stopped making any deposits and just left the sum to sit, letting the interest compound over time. When he turned sixty-five years and two months, ready to retire, his total earnings amounted to $934,461.

Buy's car, meanwhile, had long ago become scrap metal.

This is the reason why we must begin saving money and exerting self-control at an early age. Bank set aside money each month for only five years, after which he was free to use his entire monthly salary. Meanwhile the $14,601 bloomed on its own, into nearly a million dollars in 40.2 years.

(The formula to calculate how long it'll take for a sum to double itself is 72 / rate of the accumulated saving. For example, at the return rate of 10% a year, we'd calculate 72 / 10 = 7.2 years as the amount of time it would take for the sum to double itself)

To illustrate further, if I save $200,000 at 10% annual interest for my son, every 7.2 years that sum would double: from $400,000 to $800,000 to $1,600,000, and in 28.8 years it will grow into $3,200,000.

Even though the interest rates are extremely low lately; it doesn't mean that we shouldn't continue to save. Before making any purchases, stop a moment, and consider how much missed opportunities, such as beginning to save money from a young age, will cost us in the long run? This includes missing other opportunities that have nothing to do with money.

Accruing debt is one easy way to put unforeseen burden to our life. Being in debt is being in suffering, it is a merciless weight on our life. Is accruing debt worth it for what we get? We might justify taking on debt cautiously for a good reason, such as investing in our own or our children's education, or make small financial investments. If really necessary, debt should be used only for the investment that yields a much higher return than the interest rate charged, and obviously not for indulging in consumption, which gives no returns. Our perspectives on investment must be thorough, and for long-term. If we are in debt for our expensive out-of-reach homes, luxury cars, luxury expenses, and shopping sprees— none of which give back any return to help payoff our debt—we pave for ourselves a path to future misery. We may reach a point at which we reflect on our living situation, realizing that this home, this car, or this school does not suit our life at all! Let go, relax your grasp on certain things in life—the ones that drain you senselessly, and see that you truly have choices, always.

Moreover, the capital investment is not limited to just the financial, but ideas, innovations, skills, and connections, are also great start-up capital. Many successful businesses start with ideas as capital and use very little start up money. The ideas pay for themselves to grow.

This may be the right time to reconsider things we conveniently use in our life. Ask ourselves if this car or house serves us or if we serve them. Let go of some peanuts. Life offers many doors for us.

Joyful Work

During the big financial challenge in my life, it was imperative for me to provide for my son and my staff. I was deeply
concerned about the uncertainty of business.

One morning when I opened my eyes from my meditation,
the morning sun rays touched me with gentleness. I realized
then that money is not the only means of capital. Wisdom,
creativity, faith, self-respect, perseverance, flexibility, the
ability to make compromises, understanding, and attentive-
ness: all of these qualities are personal capital we can use to
create prosperity in our life outside and inside.

The single most important thing in human beings is the
quality of their minds. Nineteenth-century Scottish author and
reformer Samuel Smiles said that our thoughts determine our
actions, our actions determine our characters, our characters
determine our habits, and our habits determine our destiny.
In our inner training, we begin right at the source of our
destiny: our mind, our thoughts. We examine our thoughts
in each moment before any one of them becomes action.
We do this until such self-examining becomes a part of our
character, and consequently roots itself firmly as a personal
habit. But even better than that is when we hone our
self-awareness to such a keen edge that we rise above our
character, above our habits. When our self-awareness has
become that incisive, our wisdom becomes our guide—
guiding our actions to always be in line with our purposes
and fixing our life path on the course we have chosen the
whole way.

One thing I've discovered is that when we change, our thoughts change, and consequently our life qualities change. After I left the retreat, everyone witnessed my breakthrough— my new lifestyle, from the way I made decisions to the way I worked. I recall how everyone around me—my parents, siblings, friends, and colleagues—all began undertaking the training in self-awareness. When people understand them-selves better, they understand others better. The relationships among family members become warmer and closer, and the relationships among co-workers grow smoother.

The business we ran back then involved three small diamond stores, each located in a large department store. Within a few months, our business expanded to six locations, and another few months later, to nine. Though we could have kept expanding, we did not. Nine was enough. More than that and we'd have begun burning ourselves out, with no time for keep our minds sharp.

I recall several people asking me then, "How do you make a living in an economy like this?" I'd answer them that if I had not entered the meditation retreat and delved into the workings of my mind, there's no way my life would have made any progress. Neither would my family be happy, nor would my business be prosperous.

Every single day I am indebted to the Enlightened Buddha and the teachers of his teachings, who have shown me the freedom and happiness path, and I am now passing on this valuable knowledge to everyone.

The Essence of Work

A mindful mind knows that the essence of work is not only the paycheck and status, but also the opportunity to benefit our fellow humans and to develop ourselves. Without this realization, we limit our moment of happiness to payday and promotion time, both of which will be in decline if we don't give the genuine value to people and ourselves. Appreciating the genuine values of our work—which is to sharpen our mind, polish our understanding, groom our skills, and cultivate our compassion—we'll experience happiness at every moment. When things are easy, we prosper. When things are challenging, we learn, leap, and prosper more. We derive happiness from the period before we start our work, when we are planning—from being attentive while we work, and when the work is done we learn from the results and grow more. With the understanding of genuine values of our work, we are happy before, during, and after work. Without this understanding, people struggle to go to work, while at work, after the work is done, and especially when their earnings decline. So this route yields no good at any point along its path, but many people are unaware of this and choose it anyway.

Our happiness starts inside and when other people's lives are improved as a result of our works, we beam. Our creativity is at its best and our appreciation of our work expands.

Teachers see their students progress and they experience deep pleasure in their work. Accountants see the value of their work reflected in the efficient and precise administration of a business. The work becomes enjoyable, as they find challenges in the analysis of quarterly figures and the development of financial and corporate performance reports. Street sweepers find contentment in each stroke of their brooms—seeing the complete cleanliness of a street they have just swept, their hearts feel swept clean. The guard at the office building where my company was located, beamed each time a vehicle rolled onto the parking lot— almost sprinting towards the vehicle to direct its driver carefully into a certain parking space. On rainy days he escorted everyone to and from the parking lot with his umbrella. His smile reflected the kind of contentment he felt in his job that some executives might never experience.

One who has taught me greatly in this matter is a street vendor who sold a sweetened, iced-fruit dessert for 30 cents with such perfection. She strained the thin, sweet syrup-water to crystal clarity, hand-carved pieces of fruits, and added tiny ice cubes to make a refreshing ice dessert for hot days. Customers felt refreshed, and she herself felt delighted throughout the process. She told me, "We must be honest and honor our work."

Have you ever been to a restaurant where you feel they do not honor their creations? Our work is our masterpiece that is born of our mind. When we treat our work delicately, we are grooming our soul.

Fathers and mothers raising children are delivering their lives' masterpieces as gifts to the world. Their souls will live on in their children. What they have done for their children and the love they have given them will be passed on from generations to generations. The success of raising kind, happy children means much more than raising corporate entities. Your company can replace your position in a few days, but no one can ever replace you in your children's lives.

In the process of writing this book, I intended to write every day with enjoyment — to write, then observe my mind, then return to writing. I benefited immensely from the process. And if those who read this book notice how they feel while their eyes see these letters, and they are awakened, experience joy, take things they've read and use them in their lives, and increase their overall happiness ... then my purpose is fulfilled!

It doesn't matter what our jobs are, if we view ourselves merely as sellers of goods or services, we limit our lives by abandoning something essential. But when we broaden our perspective, our work develops our own mind and the minds of those around us. Enlightening ourselves and enlightening others through our work should be our goal. This will bring us happiness everyday of our life. The services we provide can bring happiness to our customers, fulfil their hearts, and enrich the quality of their lives and those of their loved ones. That is their purpose in obtaining the services from us. Some may choose to loathe their work and not to put their full effort into it. But that will diminish their skills and mind qualities, and the work they long for will never arrive. While those who know it is wise to maintain a happy, diligent mind before, during, and after delivering services will gain life contentment and achieve the accomplishment they deserve. The surrounding that matches their high-quality minds will manifest. We are providing happiness to people, which in turn give us the providers happiness. Through approaching our work this way, we are giving honor to what we do every moment at work, just like the aforementioned street vendor. When talking with our co-workers, we could encourage one another and point out ways to add water to our glasses, while adjusting the size of our glasses to fit our respective situations. People living in accordance with their income and purposes feel satisfied with what they have and experience contentment and satisfaction in their jobs. They do not have any debts to bear. So, their minds are at ease. They can carry out their jobs efficiently and well. The business prospers and so do they.

Looking at it from a business perspective, when there's faith and trust among a company's staff, and between the company and its customers, suppliers, and business allies—such relationships generate great creativity, business flow, and long-term relationship. This reduces the need to monitor the operations closely, which saves the company a considerable amount of money. Developing such relationships starts from within each individual. We see many people working with their hearts not in their work—no real sense of responsibility. They're not ready to provide their goods or services since there's no guidance for them to see the value of their work. So, their minds are adrift from it.

Why wait for the reward of our work to come at the end of the month in the form of a paycheck and waste the rewards from the rest of the month. Rather, our work, in and of itself, becomes the reward that brings pleasure to us in every moment of learning. Since we spend a lot of hours in life working, we should use them to nourish the quality of happiness in our life. When we are emotionally rewarded, we will also be financially rewarded.

After I started working with this understanding of the value of my work, my debt soon disappeared and there was more than enough money for my son and me. I was financially free, sold my diamond business, and moved to a house on the beach, then a house by a beautiful river. I now choose how, where, and with whom I want to work. Several times a year I also conduct meditation retreats for thousands of people. They come to stay at a beautiful resort to do their walking and sitting meditation, and go home with new wisdom and tranquil minds. On occasions, I teach life and mind management classes that transform the lives of

The Compass of NOW

What are the genuine purposes of our work? How do we benefit the lives of others?

people from all over the world. When they have themselves as their own paradise island of happiness, they can always come back to rest any time. Their love, relationship, finance, health, and daily happiness improve with the strength of their lives' purposes and the profound meaning in their daily routines.

This happens while our goal is set on inner growth. Many people ignore their inner development and speak of nothing but money. They worship only wealth and exalt profits as the driving force behind all work. Hence, they pursue their unreachable goal like a hamster keeps running in its wheel. Their profits are not mounting, but their debts are.

Our choices of paths bring our journeys and destinations.

The last thing you do the best is what you have the most joy doing.

Malcolm Forbes

Greed

Many might wonder how monitoring our mind will help us with our work. Will observing our mind and thoughts extinguish our ideas and hence our prosperity? Will we not feel like other humans?

In fact, we will be better at everything in life, including making money, when we are accustomed to seeing thoughts and ideas arise, whereas previously our mind was used to wander around, cluttered with so many thoughts that we could hardly separate out the beneficial ones. Now we can see our thoughts and consciously proceed with them, with a wider perspective of self, of the business environment, and of others.

We are still making money. What becomes different with this need is that before, when motivated by greed, all we'd focus on was getting what we wanted, like we had blinders on and there were no other ways. What we couldn't see was that we might be heading down a path leading to a big loss. Once trained, however, our self-awareness keeps us careful. When there are stirrings within us to do something, our self-awareness would warn us to check within ourselves. We would constantly examine each and every decision and think about how it will affect our life, our family, the well-being of everyone around us, and the ecology. We'd also consider the potential downside of the decision as well as its success.

The Compass of NOW

Are you thinking of doing something too big, too much, or too little? Does it fit all aspects of your life?

We'll perceive the benefits and the drawbacks of what we are about to do, and pursue a lifestyle according to a desire-glass, which has been re-sized appropriately and realistically. There's no more rushing into something too big that threatens to overwhelm us, or those close to us. We will profit internally and externally. We can also dissociate ourselves from our thoughts and clearly see the need that is driving us to make a decision. That's how we progress internally and externally.

When we want to expand our business with loans or to have business partners, we should start questioning ourselves: Why can't I do it on our own? Will my partner lessen or add to the burden of my life? Managing our own thoughts and needs is not easy, let alone manage others'. Partnerships will work when each party is self-sustaining and financially independent, with a strong mind that will not put personal need for recognition before the prosperity of business. The ego issue is harder to manage than the financial matter.

For a large enterprise with abundant resources and where the owners do not feel personally attached to the business, the expansion, merger, or acquisition may become successful. But for a small start-up business where each partner desires for success, wealth, and recognition, these developments may be harder to manage. The truth is that one-owner small enterprises have their own beauty. When we set up a business, our idea, creativity, and persistence are our capital. Be careful not to jump into a partnership hoping to impose certain responsibility we don't want to do on our partner. In general, the responsibility we try to avoid tends to come back to haunt us.

Small businesses with desire-glasses sized accordingly have advantages over large enterprises. Our assets and our expenses are kept within a manageable range. We can achieve a smooth efficiency. In this rapidly shifting world, with the complexities of globalization and economies being subject to great, unforeseen forces beyond their borders, amidst such possibilities of instability; we are small but strong and maneuverable.

As an employee of a company, receiving a salary, we manage our income and expenses with our desire-glasses sized appropriately. The things we choose to spend our money or time on, we choose according to their values to ourselves, not just because they're popular. Our life knows stability. Our stress is much less than that of business owners. At work, we continue developing our skills and our perseverance. Our co-workers feel our goodwill towards them. Each day is an opportunity to learn. All this, and we can also succeed and reach our goals daily.

I told my team every now and then that our new branches could be started up and could be shut down anytime. Whatever saps strength from our operations could always be removed to keep our business vital and healthy. It's not necessary for us to worry about keeping up the appearance that may debilitate us in the long run. The same holds true for each individual. If our home is a costly burden to us, we move to a more affordable home. If our car is a money drain, we must stop using it.

There was a retired businessman, who had guaranteed a loan for a friend. The friend suddenly left town. If the businessman had let the bank seize his friend's property and collect a modest sum from him for the outstanding loan he had guaranteed, a sum which would cause him no significant hardship, the story would have ended right there. Instead, the businessman sought to solve the problem by creating an even bigger one. He made a down payment of over a hundred thousand dollars on the purchase of his friend's property, hoping to resell it for a nice profit. Ten years passed and the property still hadn't been sold. He then concluded he must accept going into debt and borrowed a couple of million dollars to buy the property outright. The man ended up suffering a huge loss, all because he was worried about losing a modest sum of money to cover up his friend's debt (and losing some dignity with it). In the end, he lost massively in both regards. By refusing to open up his fist and let go of the peanuts, the retired businessman stubbornly maintained his grasp right into the face of harmful consequences.

Everything comes down to vigilant awareness of self. When our mind clings with an iron grip onto some thoughts or feelings, and we find ourselves unable to release them, we'll eventually feel the pain. However, when we consider any situation cautiously, we'll often find that accepting some loss or hurt to a small part of us will do us much less harm than when we deny it and allow a much more harmful situation to engulf us later on. We must be prepared to make small sacrifices of self-indulgence at the right time in order to maintain the smooth efficiency of our new sustainable lifestyle. Life without debts has no need to rush into any risky investment, especially not the one that risks the well-being of our family and loved ones.

SOULS NOT FOR SALE

Some of us may not like the business ethics or attitudes of the company we work for. We may start by considering what benefits our company gives to customers and society. If we can identify the benefits our work yield, we can appreciate that aspect of our work and accept the parts we do not like because we can also learn from them with peaceful mind. We can't expect everything to match our ways, but when we are at peace with ourselves and act in the best interest of others, our surroundings adjust themselves to match our good heart.

However, if what we're doing conflicts with our principles and morals or damages the good in our nature, we need to stop and reflect. Our work is what we spend most of our waking hours doing. If it obstructs us from realizing our inner potential, conflicts with our morals on a daily basis, we must stop, stand our ground, and reflect: Is the work we do daily at this company consistent with the path we want to follow?

The Mousetrap

Some might feel uncomfortable at work and wish to find a new job but couldn't because of their large debts, and their competence lower than their current salaries—which have been increased each year; though their skills have not improved. Therefore, no other companies will hire them at their current salaries.

Chan was an engineer in a factory. He had no pleasure from his work because he hated the factory's owner. He told me that the owner had built a fake well to treat the factory's wastewater to deceive government inspectors. His boss actually had been dumping the factory's toxic wastewater into the nearby river—the one used by villagers, including Chan's parents, for bathing, cooking, fishing, and washing fruits and vegetables. Although he despised his boss because of this, Chan did not dare to leave his job due to his uncertainty of finding a new one. It was a risk he could not take when he had a family to provide for.

If we feel that our current potential is not enough to land us a new job, we might have to start reviewing what we've been doing all along! If all the time we've spent at work do not advance us in any way, either in our inner life or our outer life; if we do not use our work as a means to build up knowledge, skills, perseverance, good will; if we do not use our work to sharpen the edges of our wisdom—then we must begin doing so from this day onwards.

Jane was a senior executive when the new ownership and management took over and made it clear to her that she should leave. But Jane wasn't able to start anew. Even though her heart desired to open her own small business, knowing that early on it'd be tough going but would improve later on; Jane still couldn't leave her present position. She carried a huge debt burden. Her large salary was just enough to cover basic family expenses as well as her mortgage, car, and credit card payments. She had to put on her grin and continue to bear the situation; although she suffered greatly.

When people live carelessly, wallow in self-indulgent shopping, or fail to invest time and energy in developing their competence, they are falling into a trap. They would find themselves trapped in the situations they loathe. Coming back to the freedom path needs courage, initial cutbacks in extravagance, perseverance, and dedication to self-improvement. Self-refinement takes time but the result lasts a lifetime.

Way Out

There is no quick fix to achieve a quality life. Start with a solid foundation. Be aware of our thoughts-what are the drives behind our actions?

Ask ourselves: Do I want to buy this to look wealthy when I would be left with less money? Do I really want to win this argument with my spouse or do I want my loved one to show me that he or she loves me? If it is the latter, then I would be better off not argue. Where will the action take my life? And do I really want to go there?

Ask ourselves what we are doing, for what, why, and how.

Consider the path we want. Strengthen ourselves internally through self-observation. Travel light with less or no debts. Broaden our perspectives. Find and polish our gifts, talents, and skills.

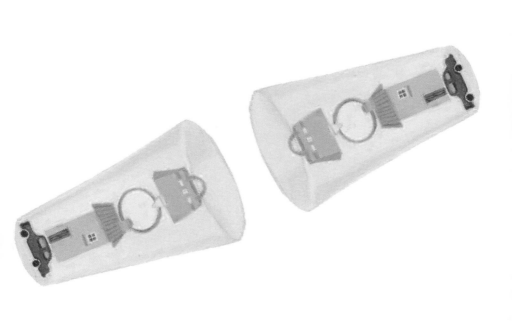

Find Ourselves

Many people go through life without realizing what they truly love, enjoy doing, or what they do well. I discovered myself through volunteer work by giving talks on how to be financially and emotionally free. From the time that I was running my diamond business and still had debts until the time I became financially free and sold my business, I gave talks, taught meditations, helped million of people find their ways out of misery. With them I shared my experiences and helped them build up the willpower to see ways out of their situations. It was work in which I discovered myself, understood myself, and, at the same time, felt deep contentment in helping others to likewise discover themselves.

We must identify the things in life we truly love and want to do. The starting point is to look for things we love, in all that we are doing now, and perform them to the best of our abilities. Use them as the starting point in discovering and harnessing the creative power that lies deep within us. Happiness begins right here, right now, in what we presently do, and where we presently are. Everything has a positive side and it is always right in front of us. The best things in life are right before us, yet we must open our mind wide to realize and receive them.

Be Real

No matter what we want to do, we must first see through it as though it's a piece of crystal in our hands. We turn it one way, then turn it another way, examine it from all angles with our own cautious mind, not through someone else's mind.

Imagine how we would take on difficult situations that may arise—keeping in mind that in real life, situations may sometimes turn out differently from what we'd imagine. Those who are able to reverse the difficult situations will become stronger and will live their lives freely and in safety. Succeeding in life does not come to one like winning a lottery—it comes through genuine good works, through the insight, through doing what is true, what is good, and what we can respect ourselves for.

A wishful thinker sees the success and wealth of others as the results of good fortunes—something that came easily. Such thinking has never helped anybody reach his or her ultimate goal.

Part 6

BE KIND IN RELATIONSHIPS

THE BASKET OF LIFE

Taking care of our mind and our family's happiness is the main value that nourishes our life, and we should prioritize and set aside our time for our values.

Suppose that today you head out in high spirit and walk to the market to do your weekly shopping. There, you see colorful toys, crunchy snacks, household appliances, sets of wine glasses, and bars of lavender-scented soap. Your desire is piqued, you buy as you stroll along, until you realize with a jolt upon reaching the meat, vegetables and fruits sections that you've used up your budget for the month, not just for this week, and you're panting and loaded up with items in both arms. Your basket is bulging from your purchasing spree. You cannot buy any more items as you have no more money and no more strength to carry them.

Our life is like this. Nature gives us a limited amount of time to walk on this earth. And we have the right to choose what we put into our life-basket and what stays out. If we're not careful, our life-basket, limited as it is in time and energy, will be filled up with things which are completely unnecessary and useless to our life. It is imperative that each of us knows for certain what is vital to our life and that we apportion our limited resources—our time, money, physical, mental, and emotional energies—by devoting them first to the things that are most vital to our well-being.

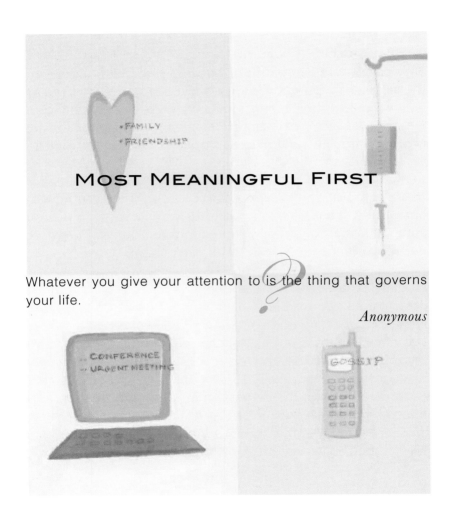

MOST MEANINGFUL FIRST

Whatever you give your attention to is the thing that governs your life.

Anonymous

Many of us might think that we've already given our top priorities their due time and energy. Yet if we carefully monitor ourselves moment-to-moment, we'll see that the bulk of our time is spent on frivolous things. We may also devote ourselves entirely to our work, reasoning that this is how we're looking after our loved ones, by working hard to maintain a high standard of living. We have to check if that is necessary and what would be the balance of the time away from family and the financial gain.

Let's be careful not to create such burdens for ourselves from our own weakness: to acquire more possessions or more debts, to work harder and harder ... just because we do not know how to spend time with our loved ones, and because we've never been hugged and held by our parents. Deviations in life cause many problems. But people still escape to deviations because they do not have the strength to look into their minds to see what they hate to admit. They rather spend time on other things that are less painful; even though those things take them further away from their goals.

When we're at work, are we killing time by responding to unimportant personal e-mails, surfing the Internet, chatting idly on the phone, letting mind adrift, and unable to focus on a task for more than ten minutes?

Even in our meditation retreat time, do we carry our things to do and our expectation to gain wisdom with us, which actually keeps us further away from it?

Prioritizing Our Life

The Eisenhower matrix, by the US president Dwight D. Eisenhower, the master of time management, talks about the four "chambers" in our mind into which the various matters of our life are placed. Which chamber each matter is placed into depends on its priority rating.

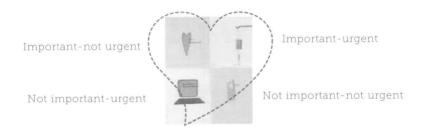

Important-not urgent

Important-urgent

Not important-urgent

Not important-not urgent

"Important-not urgent" includes such matters as life-planning, looking after our health, taking care of our family, honing our knowledge and skills, and of course, developing our wisdom. If we truly give these matters top priority, we will know enduring contentment. We often procrastinate only because our loved ones sometimes remind us of certain pains from the past. But if we can just be aware of the feeling, the fear, or even the pain, we can manage to be with our loved ones in a nurturing way, and will no longer allow other matters to capture our time and energy.

Although our children do not have their "appointments" with us fixed by a secretary—appointments to go bike riding, to lie down beside us, to read, to talk, and to play; we should place first our appointments with them—our special time for them—before others so that we won't be too tired and will be fresh and ready to be with them.

"Important and urgent" is the next chamber. If we do not properly take care of our life priorities that are important though not urgent, they will transform into the important and urgent matters, such as problems related to our physical or mental health, our marriage, or our relationship with our children. These obviously need to be taken care of immediately, and even then it might be too late to turn things around. We must take proper care of the important matters of our life while they're still in the first chamber. Then and only then will such emergencies become rare.

The Compass of NOW

What do you put all your efforts into? Is it really the most important thing in your life that deserves most of your time?

The third chamber "Not important-urgent" are things like attending "urgent" meetings that have no real point for hours each day. The fourth and final chamber, "Not important-not urgent", includes those matters that are inessential to our life, but which nonetheless are where we likely spend most of our time and energy! Chatting idly on the phone, playful texting, spacing out in front of the TV set, browsing the Internet, playing computer games, and poring over advertisement leaflets.

In managing our life, the essential rule is to allocate our time and energy first to that which is most meaningful to us. Beware of letting ourselves slip, and take up precious space in our life-basket.

The key to this is awareness and a strong sense of life's purposes and values. With our mind fixed upon our life's purposes, we know what we would do and wouldn't do, what contributes to our values, and remain watchful for when we want to deviate or escape to what is not.

With mindfulness, we will not be devoting our energy to wishing for a necklace, a paycheck, and no bills. The wishes that are made out of scarcity and inadequacy only bring scarcity and inadequacy. Instead, we first ask ourselves what really nourishes our life that we should wish for, then we can easily make those things happen because we already have them in our life. We will begin appreciating them, cultivating compassion, mindfulness, and understanding in our life, and we will receive the ultimate happiness that endures. Great things in life are always right in front of us. We just need mindful eyes to see them.

Mindfulness and compassion, not greed, are the true abundant state of mind. And abundance only brings abundance.

Clean and Clear

After a meditation retreat, in which we had focused on ridding our mind of all that were useless and detrimental and had achieved a pleasant lightness of being, we will no longer tolerate cluttered rooms, desks, or houses. Clean minds need clean spaces.

Let's open up our wardrobes. How much clothing do you see that you've never worn, and will probably never wear? Clothes you once loved wearing, but once out of your sight, would leave your mind, too. They were there all along, obscured by the clutter.

Our life can be cluttered just the same. People add to our clutter, congesting our ears, eyes, and feelings with negative and worthless content that impedes our inner development. Nevertheless, we endure it because we accustom ourselves to it. We endure daily work that wears down our spirit because we allow ourselves to get used to it. We endure ourselves, continually becoming irritable, angry, stressed, and bored. Many people, though not liking it, don't have enough strength to change. They don't want to think, don't want to face change, and come to accept defeat and live the

lives that they don't like. The same goes for what people tolerate in their physical surroundings and in their homes—each room abounding with things they hardly ever use, never mind need. It's time for us to clean the clutter out of our life.

Our mind must be strong, steady, and clear in order to sort through and determine what benefits us and what doesn't. We must expunge both internal clutter and external clutter. In order to attain the inner focus necessary to effectively cleanse the mind of defilement, we must first reduce the clutter outside us. Too much clutter in our physical surroundings will impede our self-awareness. Our heart, mind, and body are fully our responsibilities—take great care of them.

Sources Of Happiness

Our loved ones are sources of happiness that are right beside us. We do not have to buy them, we only need to have the time to enjoy each other, to learn and to share together, and to lift one another's spirit up. Our loved ones—yes, they may sometimes cause us some problems, too. Problems may arise—but do we need to be upset? Of course not. The choice of feeling is entirely upon us.

Love Incompetence

Humans always need love. Not knowing how to love leads to misery from wanting others to be a certain way.

When people love with unfulfilled hearts, they do things for the ones they love out of the need to fill in the empty spaces in their hearts. Such love is selfish and self-centered. When such love does not receive the reciprocation for which it aims, they experience great displeasure, become moody, and act and speak out rashly. Genuine love cannot bloom in such barren inner soil.

Love that is full of selfish desire is a feeling with a rough edge. It is not pure. It is a muddle of expectation, anger, and dissatisfaction. Filled with such love, people encage themselves within suffering and keep lamenting, "Why hasn't this love brought me any deep, lasting happiness?"

On the other hand, if we sense the emptiness in our heart, along with our impulsive desire to fill it, we can extinguish it by just acknowledging it. The emptiness turns to strength every time we acknowledge it. Our feelings for, and behaviors towards, others may then spring from genuinely positive desires.

Our love does not cause us to ache nor is it a burden to our loved ones. Our love is the genuine good wish. We beam with joy, our loved ones feel the glow, and they know it as love.

LOVE COMPETENCE

Marzia approached me before my talk. She showed traces of a once-elegant beauty, but her overall appearance was pale, even sickly. Her eyes were frighteningly swollen, as if she had been sobbing for days. She was a high-level executive of a major investment bank. She told me she had sensed her husband's possible interest in another woman and felt as if her heart had been ripped in half. From a stately, beautiful woman leading a successful career and exuding self-confidence, Marzia had become someone who felt worthless, as if she had lost her place in this world. Everyday, she pleaded for her husband's affection—for his love, for him to hold her, and not leave her. Even though he had confirmed his commitment to her and carried himself on as he always had; Marzia was still fearful, apprehensive each time the phone rang that it might be another woman. She persisted in pressing for verification that he loved her until gradually, he became almost estranged from her. The more she chased him, the more he shrank away. There had been the time when he used to be so proud of her and her accomplishments and loved taking her out on the town—but that time was gone.

I told her that what she had been doing was driving her husband out of her life completely. Continuing to throw herself at his feet and begging him to love her would only repulse him to the point that he'd flick her off his legs and walk away for good.

No one wants to love someone who doesn't love and respect herself. If people do not know and feel their own worth, how will others know and feel it? Everything they say, do, and think that springs from the scarcity and inadequacy in their hearts would only drive other people and good things away from them, rather than drawing those towards them.

So when people's wishes arise out of a feeling of shortage, their wishes would not be fulfilled. By adding acknowledgment of the movements of our body and mind into our daily routine, we will feel sufficient and compassionate. And the great effect is that it will draw towards us great people and things that are really good for our life.

Parents And Children

Ranee is a woman whose life appeared perfect when viewed from the outside. She, her husband, and her son, were well-respected in their community, and each of them was very good-natured. Ranee herself was extremely dedicated to her son, pouring much of her time and energy into molding him to be perfect. Everything for him had to be the best possible: schools, tutors, weekends packed with activities, lessons, and appointments. She was relentlessly strict with him in every facet of his life. Ranee held her son to the highest standards of behaviors and manners—in how he ate, played, spoke, and studied. Then one day, he approached her and told her that he hated her ... hated her for trying to impose her dreams on his life and for forcing him to do everything to feed her own selfish desires every moment and every step of his life. He then demanded to have his life for himself from that day onwards and expressed his hope that one day, once he had grown into maturity, he might return to see her.

It is imperative for us to be aware of the fear, anxiety, or emptiness that arise in us or else we will impose our unfulfilled dreams on our loved ones. No one wants to live other people's dreams. They want to choose how to live their lives. If parents force their children to fulfill the parents' dreams, the children will not take full responsibility for their lives because if anything goes wrong, they always have their parents to blame.

As parents, we need to train ourselves to be watchful of our desire to hold onto and protect our children as if they were still babies. We must be mindful of our needs and love our children the way they are. We teach them through our good deeds, take good care of them, spend quality time with them, However, how a tree grows and blossoms is not the gardener's call.

The Compass of NOW

Is your love a burden or a gift to your loved ones?

Anger

Our relationships with loved ones and with those around us sometimes involve words and actions that may stir up anger or dissatisfaction. But once we've instilled self-awareness, the instant our mind drifts and latches onto something that irritates us, we realize it. Then we can see how we have prevented a problem from arising.

Imagine it as hearing a sound. One moment we hear the sound; its waves enter our ears, our mind processes it, and anger flares up immediately. The next nano-moment, the inner flare-up will be processed into harsh words or action. But instead of that happening, our self-awareness could catch our mind, just before we burst out. The whole process, from its origin, was laid bare before our trained awareness. The origin of distress is the unobserved mind. But with prompt observation, we are the master of our mind and our life. Great people and great things are drawn to people who live in such a way because true goodness attracts true goodness, while greed attracts greed, empty people attracts empty people, anger attracts more anger, and a mindfully, blissful state of mind attracts more bliss and joy into our life.

The Compass of NOW

If you want to get back at someone, begin by getting your life back.

There is never a good enough reason to be angry and send bad energy and the chemicals resulting from anger from our brain to poison our body and mind.

If someone has no intention of hurting you, then there is no need to be angry. If someone intends to hurt you, then there is also no need for you to allow him or her to succeed in making you suffer. Anger not only harms your body and mind, it also hurts your loved ones. When we are mindful, we know well to acknowledge the rage that rises up, notice it and not allow ourselves to be consumed by it, and choose a wise action that prevents harms to our life and possessions. If you want to get back at someone, begin by getting your life back.

Anger starts from a feeling that something or someone is threatening our life, our possessions, or our goals. It touches our family, our friends, our possessions, our beliefs, or our honor. The more we're attached to what has been threatened, the more extreme the rage that'll course through our veins.

We might believe ourselves to be calm and mild-mannered, but we can all become awfully frightening. For instance, if anyone should threaten or harm our children, our loved ones, our place in our family and in society, our beliefs, or our possessions, we each have the capacity to manifest a rage of shockingly destructive force.

Let's reflect on a quarrel we might have had with our loved ones—our parents, siblings, children, spouse, or friends. It might begin as a small matter and grew worse—damaging both sides before it got any better. Relationships often fall apart due to the outbursts of anger. Despite the love that was always there—anger shoved it aside. Many of us lament, what can we do? When we lose our temper, we lose control of ourselves.

A trained awareness can lessen the effect of anger. Immediately, when we sense a vague dissatisfaction arise, a tiny smoldering, we swiftly acknowledge it before it develops into a full-momentum anger.

We see it in time for what it is: a thing separate from our mind, a guest whom the house-owner has not welcomed and who, therefore, couldn't enter our home. Maintain moment-to-moment awareness of the small flares within. We can choose to be careful with our words, our behaviors, and our mind. Beware of the superiority feeling—the feeling that we're "above" our antagonist—and beware of showing it in our body language because it might ignite hostility and escalate until we reach a point of no return. Our anger could become uncontrollable, and the damage that ensues may be irreparable.

Words cut more than swords.
Thirteenth-century proverb

The Scars That Remain

There was a boy with a terrible temper. His father had an idea. He gave his son a bag of nails and told him, "Every time you lose your temper or feel irritable, I want you to hammer a nail into our back fence — that's all."

The first day passed, and the boy hammered thirty-seven nails into the fence. Then each day that passed, the number of nails he hammered into the fence gradually dropped. The boy was coming to realize that controlling his emotions and keeping calm were easier than hammering a bunch of nails into that fence.

Then one day, having become much better at controlling himself, he told his father that he felt he didn't need to hammer any more nails into the fence because he had changed — he was no longer impetuous.

His father smiled and said, "If you truly have changed, demonstrate it to me. Each time you succeed in preventing anger from overtaking you, remove one nail from the fence."

Several more days passed, with the boy removing the nails as per his father's instructions, until the day came when all of the nails he had hammered into the fence were pulled out. Elated, the boy ran to his father, "I did it!"

His father took his hand, and said, "Come." They went over to the fence, and the father spoke. "Son, you did well. Recall what this fence looked like before the nails, and now look at it. It's not the same as it was before, is it? Mark well, son, whenever we do something fueled by strong emotion, it leaves a scar, as if we had actually cut ourselves or someone else with a knife. Saying "I'm sorry" a million times will not erase the scar or take away the pain that has been felt. If the person you've hurt forgives you, it still doesn't matter. What has happened has happened. The scars, mental, and physical impacts he carries—they may be with him forever."

Catching our anger as early as possible is what's crucial. Even if we can only catch it at the point when it has already expressed itself openly, at least that will break its momentum and end the vitriol coming from our side. Laying down our stubborn belief in our rightness is the starting point of resolving the situation, for both sides. But by clinging tightly to the belief *I am right,* we hurt ourselves and others.

Verdicts

Many people judge others through the lens of his or her own experiences, values, and moods that often are inaccurate and unjust.

No one wants to be judged and evaluated at all, if not asking for. There is no way any of us can ever know someone else to the extent we are able to truly evaluate their worth. (Never mind the important question of what standards by which to evaluate.) Every individual has personal reasons for what they do, say, and think in accordance with their experiences, their impulses, and the particular situations they happen to be in at the moment. We are able, though, to keep aware of our own judgment, especially its prejudice, and not to impose our verdicts on the lives of others.

MY HOUSE
MY FAMILY
MY HUSBAND
MY . . . . .

When we are judged or criticized by others, their words may stick on our mind for a long time. But if we constantly see our thoughts arise and vanish, our spoken words end in the air, we will understand that they have no actual weight and that the same is also true of other people's words of criticism.

While we regulate our desires, we must also regulate external factors in our life, in particular the people with whom we spend our time and energy. Are our relations with them conducive to the life goals and lifestyles we have set out for ourselves? A crucial factor in our life that may either lift us up high, or drag us down low, is the constellation of companions we keep around us—friends, teachers, spouse. We must choose them carefully, nourish good relationships, and never harm each other's life development.

The Compass of NOW

If you want to keep your shirt clean, don't ride a bike through mud. If your shoes hurt your feet, change your shoes.

BAITS

People who surround us are important to our growth, peace, and happiness. They can either restrain or expedite our life's development.

Many of us have experienced suffering in various relationships. Try taking a close look at our painful relationships and ask ourselves what kind of "bait" we've used to attract them, and what state of mind we were in when we attracted them into our own life. We'll see that a certain kind of "baits" attracts a certain kind of "fish."

Take for example, the women who like to dress to show off their bare skin as much as possible at parties and nights out on the town, they try to figure out their "bad luck" with relationships—wondering why the men they linked up with were insincere and treated them like dispensable toys. Meanwhile, their "plain" friends with "ordinary" lifestyles can find sincere, loving relationships. A guy who tends to show off his wealth may wonder why he only attracts friends who merely want to benefit from his wealth and never stand by him when he needs assistance. A woman who married her husband during a period when her self-respect was low may find that her husband treats her with no respect and flirts with other women.

Let's look at ourselves—how well have we been managing our relationships? We attract people like ourselves—people who are doing what we are doing, who like to do what we like to do. People who enjoy their alcohol will have friends who do likewise; people who enjoy volunteer work will have friends who do likewise, and so on. Therefore, what we attract into our life is our responsibility. If we want to change what we get, we must change what we offer. If we want to change our surroundings, people, work, wealth, we need to change the quality of our thoughts, and develop good qualities in our heart.

Everything—suffering, joy, the causes of problems, and the solutions—lies right in our mind. The essential task before each of us is to keep aware of thoughts and feelings as they emerge in our mind. We must cultivate awareness of our whole self while carrying out our daily tasks as best as we can. Some problems might not yet be resolvable externally. But internally, in our mind, we can resolve all problems through accepting the nature that is manifesting itself now and focusing on things we can best handle with our peaceful mind.

The causes and solutions to our life's challenges are within our mind. By realizing what we are thinking and feeling, and not being overwhelmed by it, we can awaken to other things that also are important to us, and we will clearly see our options. We can take on challenges with a peaceful mind while we pay full attention to our loved ones. No matter what we are facing, we know that it is important to be present with our loved ones.

We must be awakened to our life, to the present moment, because we have an appointment we don't want to miss with our life. Certain things cannot be immediately fixed externally, but they can be internally smoothed out right away.

The Compass of NOW

If we want to change what we get, change what we offer.

Part 7

LIVE WITH MINDFULNESS

Mind Gardeners

In our mind lies good and bad seeds: seeds of compassion, wisdom, tranquility, peace, love, perseverance, joy, as well as seeds of anxiety, depression, anger, guilt, fear, envy, and greed. The seeds that we nourish will grow and bear fruits in our life. And those that we rid of everyday will soon disappear. Whatever results we need in our life, we nourish those seeds.

The Compass of NOW

What are you growing in your garden of mind?

Sowing Inner Seeds

All that has happened to us, all that we have, and all that we are now, have their causes and effects, working in perfect alignment within each of us always. Each word, each action, and each thought is like a seed we sow in the plot of land that is our own life. If we sow negative thoughts, words, and actions, so will their consequences be of a similar nature. Negative begets negative, and positive begets positive. Just as with real plants, external factors may hasten or hinder our inner plants' growth. What is clear is that if we sow a plant with thorns, then we'll get a plant with thorns. If we sow apples, then we'll get apples.

If we knew for certain that criticizing someone behind their back one time meant the same would happen to us one hundred times; or that if we deceived someone once, we ourselves would be deceived one hundred times; or if we were unfaithful once, our partner would be unfaithful one hundred times—we would not have dared to do it! We would have been extremely cautious with what seeds we sow, what plants we nourish, in the fertile plot of land that is our life.

Many have asked, "All that we've already done in the past— they're done—and we must bear the consequences for a long time to come. This is hard to swallow because all of us have done many bad things in our past. What are we to do with that burden?"

WATER AND SALT

The Buddha once pointed out that the good deeds we've done are like a cupful of water, while the bad deeds are like a palmful of salt. One cup of water, with one palmful of salt, would be too salty to drink. But if we vigilantly monitor our mind every moment we're thinking, speaking, or doing something, we can sharply limit, maybe even completely prevent, any more salt from being added. The more we study and learn to observe our own self, the more meticulously our mind works, which in turn leads to a life filled with good deeds and contentment. As we make this training a central part of our life, the cupful of clear water will swell into a river, perhaps even into a lake. It will be the lake of purest water with but one palmful of salt, and the water is drinkable. We cannot change our pasts, but it is within our power to constitute a brighter future by acknowledging the now.

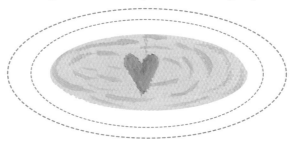

Imagine if we had accumulated one million "points" for all the good deeds we've done, yet we had to give back one thousand of them for our misdeeds. We would not be terribly troubled by this. If we had accumulated only one hundred points from good deeds and accrued a debit of one thousand points from our misdeeds though; we'd definitely be feeling the heat.

Watching over our mind is the most valuable thing each of us can do in our life. Even though some people may not even have one cupful of good karma left in their store and must face the problems to which they've led themselves; the moment they catch themselves about to plunge into the misery is the moment they can prevent it from happening. Each of us is capable of instantly lifting our own mind free of suffering.

When we've just begun our inner training, we'll likely forget ourselves and let our mind become strayed for a long period of time. But with determination to maintain vigilant self-awareness, we'll learn to observe without judgment, no pushing out and no pulling in. In the beginning, this task may seem daunting because throughout our life, we've been perpetually accumu- lating a habit of ignorance. To undo a lifetime of ignorant habit takes practice. But unlike other activities that may take a long time to bear fruits, the benefits of self-awareness are experienced instan- taneously. The moment that you are aware of yourself you feel the peace and happiness within you —an inner treasure that no one can take away from you and will always be with you.

External wealth can sometimes be taken away from us, but inner wealth always stays with us. Moreover, the inner wealth attracts sustainable wealth and success that endure.

Following are personal inner treasures that, once obtained, will result in a wealthy, healthy, and happy life:

1. Faith: Having faith in the causes and effects of all actions. We must persevere in developing our own mind, and in learning and growing from all experiences.
2. Perseverance: Efforts in watching over our mind, thoughts, actions, and words so that they do not harm ourselves or others', and efforts in lessening the impacts of past misdeeds and making sure they do not happen again.
3. Competency: Dedication to acquiring the knowledge and wisdom of life.
4. Contribution: Forgiving, giving, sharing, understanding, mercy, and compassion—a spirit of goodness that energizes others and attracts more good to come into our life.
5. Wisdom: Understanding the nature of life. Knowing what to do, how, when, where, and what for. Understanding the pros and cons of things from the observation of self and others with a tranquil mind.

Inner wealth comforts our soul. Our life becomes secure. It is the most important thing humans need to have. It attracts and secures a good life because one doesn't get what one wishes for but always gets what one deserves. We can always tend the garden of our mind to be conducive to a great life.

The Compass of NOW

Are you cultivating your inner treasure?

Chopsticks And Volcano

In Japan, there is Mount Fuji. The question is if you have to hold the volcano in a pair of chopsticks, what can you do? The question was asked and no one could answer it until one boy stood up and said, "Step back from Mount Fuji as far as you can and look through the chopsticks close to your eyes. The volcano is now in your chopsticks".

The problem is Mount Fuji.   The solution is a pair of chopsticks.

Problems in life are comparable to this Fuji volcano, and acts of solutions are like chopsticks. All we have to do is back away from the problem itself and focus on the solutions, i.e., chopsticks, not the problem. When we're focused on the solution, which is the chopsticks, the challenges get smaller, the necessary tasks get done, and our situation improves.

Examine the problem from a distance with a relaxed mind, as if the problem were someone else's. By doing this we greatly reduce the problem's size and weight. Instead of placing ourselves at the foot of Mount Fuji, or at the foot of a problem, making either one seems immense, we consider a problem from a distance.

We provide ourselves with a much broader view and thus, more options on how to best solve the challenges. There, of course, will be something we cannot resolve immediately. But by focusing our mind on the things we can do now to improve the situation, there is at least one thing we can do right away—that is to brighten up our moods and feelings, rather than to dwell on the problem and inflict the needless pain on ourselves.

The closer it is, the bigger
the problem becomes.

Focusing on solutions
shrinks the task.

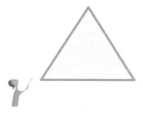

The greatest adventures are experienced in the soul... not across oceans or deserts.

Dagobert D. Runes

When I was in my teens, I asked my parents if I could go to England to study. We contacted a school, found a host family, and off I went, nervous and excited. At London's Heathrow Airport, I waited for the head of the family to pick me up as promised. She never came. So, I hauled my suitcases onto a bus, heading into the city towards my host family's house. Along the way, one of my bags, with dried, salted fish my mom had given me, somehow disappeared. Then, at the door of my host family's house, the head of the family said her son had just come home from Scotland, and she asked me to come back in two weeks or so. The door closed. I remember thinking at the time how awfully dark London's overcast sky appeared even in the daytime. Snow began falling gently and the freezing cold sank into my bones. I dragged my suitcases, headed to the school, and called home. That was the first time I shed tears inwardly.

Soon after, a Thai student I had met agreed to transfer his lease agreement on an apartment over to me and a housemate. He collected the rent in advance, took our money, and fled town. I was left to deal with the apartment owner, who insisted he could not take any responsibility for what had happened.

At that time the Thai government had also implemented strict regulations on the transfer of money out of Thailand. So, our monthly allowance came very late, and we were late in paying the rent. Our landlord then evicted us and threw all of our stuff out in front of his house—our pots, our wok, everything. He even changed the locks on the doors. That happened on New Year's Eve. I called home when everyone was celebrating in high spirits. My sister and I gathered our belongings, trudged to the railway station, and slept alongside London's homeless people.

Why didn't I just give up and return home? I look back upon that moment in my life and recall that I simply did not have the time to be in despair. I needed to focus on resolving the problems that were before me. I couldn't sit and wallow in self-pity. I thought about how I could finish what I had gone there for—my studies. Then, I could return home to do good for my country and prove to myself that the human heart can conquer anything and that persistence is stronger than any challenges.

Strengthened with meaningful purposes, our mind can focus on the meaningful goals and the tasks before us, while keeping our awareness and wisdom alert. The amount of one's happiness and success is in line with one's ability to shrink the volcano and hold it with one's chopsticks.

I have simply tried to do what seemed best each day, as each day came.

Abraham Lincoln

Last Words

All the things that have been presented in this book are simple truths, yet they require the earnest practice for their benefits to be realized.

Our mind is our most valuable asset that we need for everything in our life, and now we know how to take good care of it in order to enhance our life's true happiness.

We have ultimate potentials. All we need to do is to live with awareness of our body and mind. Our awareness is our most valuable compass—the Compass of Now. In the realization of the now, there is nothing unfavorable—just observe objects and observe our wise mind. We are in the flow of all great possibilities arising from wisdom and compassion stemming from the understanding of ourselves first and thus of nature.

Each day of our life is precious. We reflect on where our chosen acts are going to lead us to and check whether our mind is reacting against life's truths. When we form purposes and values and are true to ourselves, we pursue the path of freedom.

We must be kind in our relationships and live with mind-fulness.

Awareness is our key to happiness in all circumstances. It is our life's insurance of happiness and stability. It brings joy to the journey of life. The present moment becomes the wonderful moment of knowing we are on our chosen path. Everyday is lived as if it were the last day of our life. Be the best we can be for ourselves and our loved ones.

Looking into our mind should be our daily task, just like brushing our teeth and taking a shower. This book can become our trusted friend that always reminds us where we are heading.

Check our compass daily—observe how we are feeling and thinking, and enjoy the serenity moment of the Now. Share this knowledge with as many people as we can. The more we share the goodness, the better we become. When we are awakened, the world is a better place for our children to grow.

Things in life are impermanent, and observing the impermanence allows us to be free. We always can liberate ourselves and be happy.

May all of us be liberated ... be liberated ... be liberated.

May all of us be free.

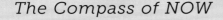

The Compass of NOW

Have you checked your compass today?

DDNARD :
THE COMPASS OF NOW AUTHOR

The healer of millions. Her books have been sold more than 1.4 million copies. She heals wounds, dries tears, brings families back together, puts smiles back on people's faces, and inspires strength in their hearts.

At 20: Graduates University of London, Master of Science in Economics.
At 25: Starts her own diamond business.
At 27: In Newspaper for her inherited debt of $3 million when her husband passed away while their baby was 11 months old. She then went into insight meditation for several years and became one of Thailand's most respected spiritual teachers. She practiced meditation deeply and managed to pay off all her debts within two years.

At 35: Retiring from diamond business, she moved to live at a beach house then at a river house with her son and started the writing of Compass series books as her wisdom gifts to people that touch hearts and warm souls. Her books became a phenomenon and have been Thailand's best selling books to date. Since then, she has been invited to give her insights on hundreds of TV shows, in magazines, and to organizations.

Every month she teaches three-day and seven-day classes on Compass Mind Management (CMM), which combines Eastern and Western healing methods for long-lasting happiness and success. People from around the world have had their lives transformed, learned to forgive their parents, others, and themselves, stopped repeating the vicious cycles of mistakes of their parents and themselves, unleashed their full potential, and lived life with a purpose.

DDnard also conducts her charitable Compass Meditation Retreats four times a year at a mountain resort in Thailand, where hundreds of participants come to meditate and everything is paid for by her special charity fund.

For busy working people, she conducts free Happiness Compass Seminars four times a year, where thousands of people come to learn how to forgive their parents and themselves, stop repeating the same mistakes, and move on to live happy and successful lives.

And for less fortunate people like inmates, physically challenged people, and flood victims, DDnard gives Compass Inspirational talks to lift up their spirits.

Today she leads a quiet life on the beautiful riverbank of Bangpakong, Thailand, meditating, gardening, and playing with her son.

COMPASS MEDITATION RETREAT

COMPASS HAPPINESS CHARITY

COMPASS OF HOPE
AT WOMEN'S CORRECTIONAL FACILITIES

COMPASS MIND MANAGEMENT CLASS

NOTES

what

when

AUTHOR : DDnard
ILLUSTRATOR : Suporntip C.
EDITOR : Pafun Supavanich
ENGLISH LANGUAGE TRANSLATING TEAM :
DDnard, Trit Napattalung, Kevin Whiston
ART DIRECTOR : Woraporn Promputra
COMPUTER GRAPHIC : Kanuengnij Sivasakul
EDITING TEAM : Sarah Wildsmith, Wendy Rohm,
Chutima Poom Kusol

CONTACT AUTHOR :
E-MAIL : compassbook@gmail.com
behappycompass@gmail.com
YOUTUBE : www.youtube.com/compassbook
www.youtube.com/compassnlp
FACEBOOK : www.facebook.com/compassofnow
www.facebook.com/DDnard
INSTAGRAM : DDNARD
WEBSITE : www.compassofnow.com, www.ddnard.com
POSTAL ADDRESS : 64/2 Mu 7, Tasa-arn,
Bangpakong, Chachengsao, 24130 Thailand
or DDNard c/o Chait S. 147 Vernon St., Malden, MA 02148, USA

PUBLISHED BY : The Life Compass Co.,Ltd.
64/2 Mu 7, Tasa-arn, Bangpakong,
Chachengsao, 24130 Thailand
Printed in Canada
DISTRIBUTED BY : Perseus Distribution 1-800-343-4499

ISBN 978-0-578-12139-0
first published in Thai in 2004
first published in English in 2013